ST
JOURNALIST

UNDERSTAND &
REPORT THE NEWS
IN YOUR COMMUNITY

STREET JOURNALIST

UNDERSTAND & REPORT THE NEWS IN YOUR COMMUNITY

LISA LOVING

MICROCOSM PUBLISHING
PORTLAND, OR

STREET JOURNALIST
Understand and Report The News In Your Community

Part of the DIY Series

© Lisa Loving, 2019

This edition © Microcosm Publishing, 2019

First Edition, 3,000 copies

First published April , 2019

ISBN 978-1-62106-107-6

This is Microcosm #214

Book design by Joe Biel

For a catalog, write or visit:

Microcosm Publishing

2752 N Williams Ave.

Portland, OR 97227

(503)799-2698

Microcosm.Pub

To join the ranks of high-class stores that feature Microcosm titles, talk to your rep: In the U.S. **Como** (Atlantic), **Fujii** (Midwest), **Book Travelers West** (Pacific), **Turnaround** in Europe, **Manda/UTP** in Canada, **New South** in Australia, and **GPS** in Asia, India, Africa, and South America.

If you bought this on Amazon, I'm so sorry because you could have gotten it cheaper and supported a small, independent publisher at *Microcosm.Pub*

Global labor conditions are bad, and our roots in industrial Cleveland in the 70s and 80s made us appreciate the need to treat workers right. Therefore, our books are MADE IN THE USA and printed on post-consumer paper.

Library of Congress Cataloging-in-Publication Data

Names: Loving, Lisa, author.

Title: Street journalist : understand & report the news in your community / Lisa Loving.

Description: Portland, Oregon : Microcosm Publishing, 2019.

Identifiers: LCCN 2018033617 | ISBN 9781621064299 (paperback)

Subjects: LCSH: Citizen journalism. | Online journalism.

Classification: LCC PN4784.C615 L68 2019 | DDC 070.4/3--dc23

LC record available at https://lccn.loc.gov/2018033617

MICROCOSM · PUBLISHING

Microcosm Publishing is Portland's most diversified publishing house and distributor with a focus on the colorful, authentic, and empowering. Our books and zines have put your power in your hands since 1996, equipping readers to make positive changes in their lives and in the world around them. Microcosm emphasizes skill-building, showing hidden histories, and fostering creativity through challenging conventional publishing wisdom with books and bookettes about DIY skills, food, bicycling, gender, self-care, and social justice. What was once a distro and record label was started by Joe Biel in his bedroom and has become among the oldest independent publishing houses in Portland, OR. We are a politically moderate, centrist publisher in a world that has inched to the right for the past 80 years.

TABLE OF CONTENTS

Introduction • 9

1 • Street Journalism House Rules • 13

2 • Is This a Story? • 17

3 • Fake News, Brain Farts, and Crap Detectors • 33

4 • Information Gathering • 49

5 • Interviewing Tips • 67

6 • What Is Investigative Reporting? • 87

7 • Pulling It All Together and Telling the Story • 103

8 • Fact-checking • 119

9 • Creating Your Voice as a Journalist • 135

10 • Platforms: Building Your Place in the Journalism World • 153

11 • Conclusion • 175

ACKNOWLEDGEMENTS

This book is dedicated to Riverbend, the "girl blogger" from Iraq. On her blog, Baghdad Burning[1], which she created after the U.S. launched our war against her country in 2003, Riverbend's stories of life and death inspired me and thousands of others around the world. It is still not known who she really is, but we do know she survived.

In her final blog posting in 2013, Riverbend wrote: "We're learning that the leaders don't make history. Populations don't make history. Historians don't write history. News networks do. The Foxes, and CNNs, and BBCs, and Jazeeras of the world make history. They twist and turn things to fit their own private agendas."

This book is also dedicated to the KBOO Community Radio Evening News and Public Affairs crew; Dingo Dismal and Olive Rootbeer; and Lanita Duke of Grassroot News. Here's a salute to visionaries, builders, and great communicators yet to come.

Biggest thanks to my family, especially David Lichtenstein, Lela Loving Lichtenstein, and James Lichtenstein, who never mocked me as I developed the Kitty Litter Theory of newsroom organization, not even once.

This book would never have happened without inspiration from Peggy Holman, Dr. Michelle Ferrier and their crew at Journalism That Matters. They sit smart, compassionate people next to each other and turn on the lightbulbs over everybody's heads.

1 Baghdad Burning, http://riverbendblog.blogspot.com (accessed October 25, 2017)

INTRODUCTION

For too long now, a big misunderstanding has hijacked the truth about what journalism is, what it's for, and who should do it. While many people believe there is some sort of special degree or license that makes a journalist "legitimate," the truth is that anyone with the interest, brains, and organization can make a crucial difference with their voice. Do you see injustice in the world? Do you want to do something about it? If you have a smartphone, then you have the basic equipment to report what is going on—live!—from the scene of wherever you are. In this book, you'll find tips on the basics of gathering news and interviewing sources, as well as navigating ethical questions and difficult situations. I'm a professional who's been there, and I'll guide you through it with step-by-step instructions, resources, and stories from the field. Frankly, I can't wait to see what you come up with.

You've heard it before: History is written by the winners. That means the powerful people in control tend to shape how we all look at ourselves over time. But that's not the whole story.

Every generation of every community of human beings on Earth has included storytellers—people who are drawn to collecting information and trying to make sense of it for others, in one way or another, sometimes as a profession. In ancient West Africa, these people were traveling wise men called "griots," who went from village to village sharing the news of the day and collecting more news as they went. In medieval Italy, they were the wandering theater troupes of the "commedia dell'arte," which did the same thing griots did but with music and comedy and costumes. In some ways you could say our modern storytellers are the talking hairdos on cable TV news channels. But not all the stories that should be told always get told.

That's why there's also always been everyday people who, one way or another, have done the same work—collecting the information that others need to know and then putting it back out through informal networks, religious events, or even "the grapevine." Whatever you want to call it, street journalism is essentially as simple as bringing important facts together, making sure they're accurate, and then making them available to a community in the form of a story people can understand. Can you see yourself interviewing the mayor of your town? Do you love experimenting with video on your phone? Do you ever look up more information about issues you see in your social media stream? Is there something you know a lot about? Maybe you're the kind of person who can't stop watching what goes on around you while you're walking in your neighborhood or riding the bus, and you see something that makes you think: What the hell just happened? Or maybe you notice people and events that connect with an issue of the day—right on the block where you live or work or go to school. You think about the history of a specific issue, the people you know who are hurt or helped by it, which includes maybe even you and your loved ones. You think: I wish the whole world could see this from the ground up, and I know just how I'd tell the story if I was in charge.

I'm here to say: You should be a street journalist; maybe you already are. Here are some tips to get out there and have a positive impact!

My goal in this book is to offer everyday people the tools to go into your communities and then educate the world about what's going on in your zone. I want to walk you through the basics of essential journalism and information-wrangling, using my own experience. This book also makes the case for a code of ethics for anyone blogging or vlogging or producing radio or anything that you want other people to consider "news."

If you have a burning story, or a curious nature, you can create your own meaningful coverage about what matters using the skills and the ethical values in this book. You don't need a grand plan; telling stories with the video button on your handheld device can be powerful, if you know how to do it. Eight-second video loops, square pictures, words on a page—it's safe to say almost anything that brings you joy to create could be a compelling tool for social and personal change. None of us knows how we will be getting the news a decade from now; I, for one, hope we still get news—fingers crossed. That's why we need more people to pick up the skills, sharpen their ethics, and decide how it's going to be done, rather than sitting around and watching other people do it.

All throughout the history of news, people started businesses, nonprofits, even radio and TV stations, with no experience. It is my hope that this information lights a fire inside those of you who have no idea you might be future media pioneers, forging stronger communities and a more just world.

Thanks for reading.

CHAPTER 1

STREET JOURNALISM HOUSE RULES

Journalism is a powerful tool. By collecting important information together and making it available in a systematic way to people who can use it, journalism weaves together the fabric of our societies. It can bring justice to marginalized communities—or it can drop innocent individuals in the jaws of vicious public opinion. Good journalism can hold powerful people accountable and shift unjust systems; bad journalism can destroy lives and destabilize nations. I am here to ask you personally: If you pick up the tools of street journalism, please use them to build, not destroy. Begin your journey with a sense of fraternity and positivity, not a taste for greed or revenge. Take pride in work that is fair and accurate. You have almost certainly picked up this book from a sense of purpose and urgency, and that's great. Stay positive.

With this perspective in mind, here are some fundamental ground rules:

- If you're not fact-checking, it's not journalism.
- Be aware of the difference between news reporting and opinion writing. Don't confuse the two.
- Sometimes journalism has a strong element of advocacy. If your vision for street reporting involves some call to action, be up-front about explaining why you're doing it, what you want people to do, and how others can help.
- Be an advocate for everyday people.
- Real information is better than opinions.
- Never make shit up.
- Never make shit up.

- No rage-tweeting or screaming in anger at people on the phone, in person, or in the digital world whatsoever.
- Think twice and then a third time about how your reporting will impact every individual and organization named in your story; make it a priority never to impact innocent people with your work.
- If you're not fact-checking, it's not journalism.

CHAPTER 2

IS THIS A STORY?

STORY

I n this section, you will learn how to sort through information to decide whether something is worth reporting about. We'll also dive into where to find story ideas; how to find sources for your stories; and we'll start to look at journalistic ethics, which are the moral judgments that come into play while you are reporting on the issues of the day.

YOU WILL LEARN:

- The basic dynamics of any story:
1. People
2. Doing something
3. For a reason

   That means you're looking around for people who are doing interesting things so you can explore their reasons and motivations. Or, you're looking for important issues, then finding out who is involved in them.

- How to set up your own system of "sources"—people to interview for stories—and how to create relationships that help you stay ahead of the issues you want to cover.

- The meaning of the legal terms "libel" and "slander"—these are two ways you can get yourself in moral, ethical, and legal trouble with any journalism project you do.

- Journalism can be a surprisingly emotional roller-coaster ride! Here are tips on maintaining a healthy you as your big journalistic projects roll out over time.

Okay, you've decided to become a street journalist. Where do you start? What makes something a good news story and how do you know where to find it? You notice all kinds of things every day that you think should be reported somewhere, somehow. But what makes something news? One good way to decide is to think in terms of issues—the big topics, or even problems that you see in your zone. A news story is not just one situation that one person or family is dealing with, but rather the bigger issue that involves a lot more people. This includes the kind of nightmarish systems or dynamics that can take over one person's life—like being evicted from a home or sexual assault or identity theft—that are beyond that one individual's control, but as a journalist you might ask: How many people suffer from that same situation? Sometimes it's a lot.

Journalism is like an information factory. Do you have a pile of facts and ideas that can influence people's lives today? Another way of looking at it is, do you have a pile of information that's of interest? What effect does it have on society?

When Michael Brown was killed by a Ferguson, Missouri, police officer in 2014, the story started out in local media as a street crime gone wrong. But local people, including one neighbor who witnessed the entire event and live-tweeted it, saw it as part of a larger pattern of racial profiling and unfair treatment by police. As it turned out, the pattern fed a city financial system that trapped thousands of people in St. Louis County in a cycle of debt to the local government. Eventually, the story came out that through the fines African-American people paid for bogus police citations, a system of racial harassment by police officers actually propped up the entire local government, including the City of Ferguson.

A story like the one about Ferguson, Missouri, is called enterprise reporting. It just means looking around your zone and thinking about situations and systems that impact a lot of people but don't make sense to you. As a street journalist, you start digging into why that is, who is impacted by it, and what they're doing about it. You can see how curiosity itself becomes one of your sharpest tools as a reporter.

How Will You Tell This Story?

Many books have been written defining what constitutes a story. It depends on what kind of tools you're using—video? Audio? Photography? Printed word? But any way you do it, there is widespread agreement on the basic parts of any story: People, doing something, for a reason. The best have action, compelling characters, and some kind of stakes—a sense of something at risk. You may decide that an object is an important piece of news—there's a new model of DeLorean sports cars!—but just the same, your report will be boring unless you make it about people.

Think about a journalism project you would like to do. Who is it about? What are they doing or not doing? Why? Take a minute to think about your favorite stories—whether they are novels, movies, or news items—and try to break down the action using that format. If you are the kind of person who hates formats, go ahead and do your own thing, but if it doesn't work, come back to this format and see if you can find and fix what's wrong with your story.

Civil Rights Reporting

Remember: The word "news" means covering issues that impact a lot of people, not just one person. There are countless ways issues can have effects on communities, but as a journalist, you should be able to see that wherever you go, people are impacted differently depending on whether they have privilege or special rights, based on their race or how rich they are or both.

As an area of reporting (and law), this is called civil rights, and it is an endless fountain of journalism that matters. If you're thinking about reporting on discrimination in the U.S., there are two key aspects of any story. You must find out, in the situation you are talking about right now, if:

- someone has been treated differently than other people or groups in the same situation, or
- a person or group is part of a community that has, down through history, suffered from discrimination, as it is defined by federal law.

The U.S. Civil Rights Act of 1965 lays out our national laws against discrimination, check it out when you're thinking about important stories you might do.

"Solutions Journalism"

A story can also be newsworthy if it shows everyday occurrences through a new lens. Solutions journalism is an interesting example of that. It's information-gathering and reporting that stresses not just issues, but specifically government and community responses to issues. Solutions journalism starts by asking: Is someone trying to fix this social problem? How is that working? Should something else be done instead? One of the most important aspects of a reporter's job is to be a watchdog for the public interest. As you are looking around your community for stories to cover, you might keep your eye on situations where public attention might have a positive impact.

Finding Sources

The first rule of news is that not all information is created equal; primary or original sources are the best, and the further a piece of information gets from its source, the less valuable it is. The second rule of news is that every piece of information should be backed up by at least three primary information sources, such as an official document, videotape, photo, a witness, or any documentation created when the event took place. As you think about reporting on some interesting issue or situation in your community, also consider what and who can give you information about what you're covering. Are there college professors, or members of the small business community, or perhaps is it a situation where teenagers are the experts?

Think in advance about who you would need to speak to for an informed take on your story, and then brainstorm about how you will contact them. Experts can often be contacted through their social media pages, or their university or company webpages. As you are looking up these people, places, and things connected to the project you are thinking about, make some kind of note on the people and organizations you are checking out, whether that's on paper or your phone or tablet or computer. Whichever tool you use, make sure you can retrieve this information later—you'll need it.

Think About Specifics

These three stories could be investigated in almost any town. Can you think of others?

Every day, when you ride public transit to work, transit police are checking the tickets and IDs of black and Hispanic teenagers—no one else, only the black and brown teenagers, day in and day out. You think: Isn't that against the law? Look for individuals and families you may know or people on social media who are going through group racial profiling by police. Will victims share their paperwork on their legal cases with you? Find the spokesperson for your public transit agency by searching news articles and the agency's website, and email your questions to that person and make your interview requests with them too. Look online for similar cases in other parts of the nation or the world. Search for lawsuits on that issue.

It's a special event for a friend. You buy something for them online and pay an extra few bucks to mail the gift by a certain date; you find out the item arrived three days late even though you paid for "expedited shipping." A quick check of the online seller's rating system reveals thousands of rage-posts by customers who say the same thing happened to them. Why isn't this being reported on and analyzed anywhere? Sources: Check Yelp—it will blow your mind the things you can learn about a business (using a healthy dose of skepticism). I always check Yelp ratings when I'm sussing out a business. Do a quick online search on lawsuits relating to this issue. Check your own social media circles to see if you know anyone who's been through it.

Your friend just opened a new cafe featuring the food their grandparents cooked, or produced a new line of personally designed clothing, or a new music collection. Isn't there somebody somewhere who reviews stuff like that? Hell yeah: You. Sources: Your social media would be key on this one.

Advocate for Everyday People

One last story source is people who look you up because they are stuck in a tough situation with the government or a corporation. This is called consumer reporting. The fact is, there are many people who need an advocate, but not enough people are in a position to help them out. Here are a few possible angles that you yourself might have already thought about, plus a couple possible sources for each story.

The Historical Lens

Another important tool to use when deciding if something is a good story idea or not is to simply dig out the background. Is there an important history behind this person, place, or thing? Where I live, so many new people are moving in all the time that many people have no idea about important events, even within the past decade. In many cases, historical stories get both new residents and old-timers all excited. Is there a gigantic luxury condominium development being built on an old abandoned battery factory? Chances are, all the people at the neighborhood senior center are talking about it over lunch right now. Go ask them!

Talk to People

We're still talking about how to find stories right? The single most important place stories come from is people. For me, that especially means people who call up and ask you to help them out of a jam where they're being squeezed by a corporation, or a bureaucracy.

Most of the time, each of those people asking for your help will have a stash of documents that you can only get directly from them, because the federal law that regulates public documents, the Freedom of Information Act, severely restricts what the public is allowed to know in many subject areas (more on that in "What is Investigative Reporting"). In my experience, the documents that everyday people have saved up through battling some terrible bureaucracy are documents that you would not even have access to through official channels. Whenever you have a source who is bringing a big pile of documents to you for the purpose of writing some important story, treat that person with the utmost honesty and care. In many cases they are vulnerable, private individuals who sacrifice a lot by bringing their conflict out into the public; this is especially true in stories about families.

It's also my experience that by the time someone who needs an advocate gets to my office, they've already been through two or three other media outlets and been turned away. So many online news outlets don't have a front door that everyday people can come through and ask for help. Virtually every one of the most impactful stories I have ever worked on walked into the front door of my office, with people sometimes dragging a rolling suitcase full of documents behind them.

Cutting Through the Noise

As you think about what you want to report on, and how to do it, you might find yourself becoming confused by the large amounts of material that start piling up. Charts, interviews, story links, videos. You are completely overwhelmed. No worries! The best way to tame a gigantic pile of information is to use one single fact from within it.

What is the single most important thing your neighbor or your mom needs to know about this pile of information? Another way of looking at it is: Who cares? Or: Why does this matter? The answer could be a shocking fact, or could be a funny fact, or just so important that it stops readers cold—what my colleague Brent Walth calls a "killer fact."

You get the idea. The single fact approach can help you over and over, because as you break down all the research you have for your project and you identify wider areas of focus, you will keep coming back to that same question: What is the single most important thing to know about this pile of facts?

Building Out the Story

Next, ask yourself: What affects that fact? You might be looking at a newly diagnosed mental health issue, or the economics of nail salons. Research how the systems work within your zone, especially the money and any politics or personal connections. Keep hammering at the most fascinating fact and pay attention to all the information that comes of it, because that is likely the framework of your future reporting.

Finally, figure out a key question that needs to be asked about your fascinating fact, based on all your background research.

Put On Your Tool Belt

Next, write that key question you have decided on at the top of some sort of document and brainstorm all the tools that you might have to unpack and look closer into. List the software, hardware, skills, and any sort of human help that will become part of your project model. Video, photographs, interviews, social media posts. Use your networks. Maybe you'll be able to do everything with your smartphone, YouTube channels, and social media posts. People, smartphone, social media—this is your digital zombie apocalypse team.

Thirdly, do a five-point web search on keywords relating to your story—plug in your best words and check the first five hits you get. Write it all down. The purpose here is to figure out key issues emerging within the field you're interested in, whether it's use of butter in dessert recipes, the damage bungee jumpers do in Zion National Park, or best practices in cat psychology. When you're looking things up, also check the images search and the video search—you will be surprised at the leads you get there.

Ethics

There are so many books out there about journalism ethics, it could sink a battleship. Please see "Street Journalism House Rules" at the beginning of this book.

We'll get more into libel and slander later, but for now the most basic ethical guidelines are: Never use journalism to improve your personal profit in a business deal; never use your position as a journalist to profit professionally or financially by discrediting or attempting to discredit a rival or someone you have a grudge against.

I would like to take this opportunity to strongly suggest: Never use the news as a tool of personal revenge. There are actual laws in the U.S. against gathering information on people's personal lives, particularly where it can be shown that the person gathering the information intends harm in some way. Don't use your personal power to lean on one person; focus on the system rather than the bureaucratic puppets within it. Dismantle the structures of evil without being a destructive asshole.

A Word on Self-Care

As you are documenting histories and stories of things that are happening in your own community, depending on what that is, the event you are writing about might be traumatizing to yourself and others. You need to take care of your own self, remaining aware when you are getting beaten down by the stories you're trying to tell.

No one will be able to take care of you except you, so adopt healthy habits if you want to have a long career in community journalism.

Reporting on the police shooting of a young man named Aaron Campbell was a journalistic turning point for me personally. In this case, an African-American man was killed by police after becoming despondent over the death of his brother that day from a chronic heart condition. His family called the police for a welfare check because they thought Campbell might kill himself.

But when law enforcement arrived, they came in large numbers and wound up in an armed standoff with Campbell. Even as one officer negotiated him out of his apartment, another officer—not wearing his communications earpiece—began shooting at him. That, in turn, prompted Campbell to run away from the shooting officers. Within seconds, he was shot to death by police, tasered, and bitten by police dogs. He was unarmed.

When it was finally made available, the police report on the incident was more than 500 pages long. There were soul-crushing details inside those pages. It took police officers more than half an hour to allow emergency medical technicians to examine Aaron Campbell, and by then he had died. Could he have been saved with more prompt medical attention? Instead, the medical examiner's report indicated that as Campbell died, he felt the sting of taser prongs, the pain of automatic gunfire, and the teeth of a police dog biting his leg—all at once. Over a period of several months, I waded through hundreds of boring documents, repetitive testimonies, and occasionally horrific details of what happened at the beloved young man's death scene. I spoke with his cousins who called the police. I couldn't sleep for weeks. I drank too much booze; I didn't want to eat.

Don't let this happen to you! When the airplane starts to dive, go ahead and put the oxygen mask on yourself first. Do you find yourself unable to sleep? Are you drinking too much? Just plain cranky and worried all the time? There are tried and true ways to sort these issues out: Create a regular exercise plan, drink less booze, take time off without a computer. Take care of yourself, and if that works out, then get back to whatever you were doing.

EXERCISES

- Brainstorm a three-point system for deciding whether to cover a story that can become your own personal plan. Make it specific. You might think: Situations on public transit, involving people in mental health crisis, receiving police citations. *Boom*—three criteria. Or: Local eateries, with locally-grown raw ingredients, prepared by chefs of color. *Boom*—three criteria. Go write your stories!

- Brainstorm a list of three issues you think should be covered that you have not seen reported in depth anywhere. For each story, can you break down in one sentence a crucial fact that would make that story worth covering?

- Find the city council meeting minutes in your area on the Internet. Page through the items on the upcoming agenda, and ask yourself: Number one, what seems to be the most exciting agenda item? Number two, does any agenda item have the police bureau's name attached to it? Number three, by clicking through the agenda attachments, can you find what is the biggest dollar amount discussed at this city council meeting, about any topic? Now, go back and do the same thing with the archived agenda items for the city council for the previous three weeks. Are there any patterns?

CHECK IT OUT!

Professor Clemencia Rodriguez put the modern concept of "street' media" on the map, starting with her book *Fissures in the Mediascape*, published in 2001. Rodriguez' classic 2011 study about her native country, Colombia, *Citizens' Media Against Armed Conflict: Disrupting Violence in Colombia* (University of Minnesota Press), describes the role of everyday people using the tools of media to help protect their own local communities from political violence.

"When grassroots communication media are deeply embedded in their communities, truly open to collective participation, and responsive to immediate and long-term local communication needs, they strengthen the agency of the community as it responds to armed violence." --Clemencia Rodriguez, *Citizens' Media Against Armed Conflict: Disrupting Violence in Colombia*

STORY IDEA:

Grocery Store Shakedown

This is a classic story that used to be called the "market basket." The reporter draws up a list of the ten most important grocery items for a common household, then travels to a bunch of different stores to compare the prices. While comparing prices at different grocery stores, reporters sometimes note patterns in outdated and spoiled food, or other things. You can focus on one particular item's pricing or price changes over time. You see this story a lot around the cost of smartphones. Market basket is a tried-and-true story; you could tell it in pictures or video or almost any platform.

TECHNIQUE

Get It Together

Create structure at the start. In deciding what to tackle on your first story, I suggest these steps:

- Decide on one subject area or issue that really interests you and commit to spending a little bit of time learning everything you can about it. Go to the Internet and type in basic words about your interest; check the top five hits you get back to see what they say.

- Now, figure out the one, single most important thing for people to know about your given subject or situation. Write it down. Take that one important thing and boil it down to one sentence. Write that down.

- Now consider for yourself: What are the next two or three most important things that your audience should know about that specific thing you flagged as most important? Write them down.

TECHNIQUE

Reporters' Rights

Around the world, journalists are believed to have certain rights to gather information and put it back out without being arrested or beaten or killed. Really though, these rights are theoretical. Even if you do "have the right," there are plenty of times you can expect to land in jail while attorneys sort it out later.

Laws regarding the rights of journalists are like patchwork around the U.S. and around the world, so research your area by web-searching lawsuits on free speech and freedom of information. A few organizations around the world support reporters who get in hot water with governments. One of the oldest is the Committee to Protect Journalists, based in New York, NY, which publishes the annual list of journalists murdered in the line of duty around the world.

Take the time to research journalism organizations in your region and see if you can hook up with a wider support group. The Society for Professional Journalists, the Online News Association, the National Association of Black Journalists, and Investigative Reporters and Editors are all longtime organizations that might give you support you need in journalistic tangles. Look them up.

CHAPTER 3

FAKE NEWS, BRAIN FARTS, AND CRAP DETECTORS

"Our comforting conviction that the world makes sense rests on a secure foundation: our almost unlimited ability to ignore our ignorance." —Daniel Kahneman, *Thinking, Fast and Slow*

As you begin using the tools of street journalism, you might think you're going up against the biggest media in the world—but that's far from true. Actually, the way our media industry operates has fundamentally changed over the past generation, as societies of all kinds have rapidly shifted from finding important information through a handful of tools—the television, the radio, and the newspaper—to digitally connected handheld devices that can also purchase consumer goods with the click of an icon. As major new giants of media industry have risen—Google, Facebook, Amazon, to name a few—they have created new systems raking in advertising profits by selling consumer goods embedded in news and information websites. And just like the cigarette makers of old, the web giants are working overtime to make their pages as addicting as they can.

While there have always been news manipulation and downright errors throughout the history of the news media, the U.S. presidential campaigns of 2016 marked a turning point in modern media around the world. That's not because of the news itself— whether the candidates lied or not—but rather, how the gigantic corporations that control so much of global Internet infrastructure created its digital advertising infrastructure. That infrastructure has made it more profitable for media entrepreneurs to make up wild political stories and post them online than to actually create content through real journalism. That is the system we see today, and that's why your work as a street journalist can make a difference in your community—if you can succeed in digging out and publishing important information that people need.

In this chapter, we'll take a look at the fake news industry, media manipulation, and a few of humankind's own flaws in logic that make fake news so common.

We'll also show you the parts on an industrial-strength crap detector, and give a few tips for sharpening the blades on yours.

YOU WILL LEARN:

- How to be aware of what you do know—and what you do not know
- How to trace the source and timeline of every piece of information—where you got it, who else has shared it, and where it originally came from
- How to understand what "fake news" is. We also need to look at the opposite: real news that everyday people do not want to see or hear
- How to, as a journalist, take steps to control your own perception of reality, before you even set out to present it to the rest of the world

You get out of bed and start scanning the morning headlines. The Democrats are trying to impose Islamic law in Florida. A teenager vacationing in Georgia finds a ghost photobombing her selfie. Texas Senator Ted Cruz's father helped kill President John F. Kennedy. You don't trust what you're reading, so you take a minute to look up some of these things and discover that the Islamic law story and the thing about Ted Cruz's' dad are not true; on the ghost photo—who knows what happens when we die?

Meanwhile, you get a text alert that says Jackie Chan is dead; this has already happened to him—on the Internet—twice. He's not dead this time either.

You start looking up Jackie Chan movies, then books, then silly plastic action figures. For the next week, an option to buy silly Jackie Chan action figures pops up in the edges of your email account every time you log in.

Meanwhile, you still need an industrial-strength crap detector just to figure out whether your favorite celebrity is dead or just "Twitter dead."

A lot of people do not realize that the Google and Facebook corporations have changed the way we all get news. They've also changed the way advertising is bought and sold. Today, there is an entire media industry built around pumping out wrong information—fake news—because the automated advertising systems created by gigantic web companies have made it profitable.

The ads themselves are programmed to follow you, personally, around the Internet, based on the trail you leave as you're clicking around the web. This programming is called the "algorithm."

It's just like Laurence Fishburne's red and blue pills in *The Matrix*—this is the blue pill, the easy one; it only shows you what you think you want to see, but someone else is controlling it. It's why your computer and phone keep showing you that same pair of purple glitter fake Ugg boots from BlahBlah-dot-com that you really wanted but didn't buy because you couldn't afford them. You must have clicked on them half a dozen times, thinking about how cool they were. Now a picture of the purple glitter fake Ugg boots and a link to the ordering page keeps appearing on your email wall and on your Facebook. If you've shopped for watches, then it's watches. If you were shopping for gorilla suits—guess what?

That's why during the 2016 presidential election in the U.S., fact-checking expert Craig Silverman, founder of Regret the Error, reported that fake news stories gained more audience traction—shares, comments and "thumbs ups" —than real news did. The stories were targeted at people who shared them with such gusto that they took on a life of their own, like a digital hurricane, earning millions and millions of looks at the Google and Facebook ads embedded in the pages. Because at the end of the day, it is all about the ads, not the politics.

Meanwhile, denial of the rate police kill unarmed black people and the denial of human-caused climate change are non-factual points of view that still dominate the conversation when bigwigs talk about public opinion and government policy.

Why? To really understand what "fake news" is, we also need to look at the opposite—real news that people simply do not want to see or hear. A lot of people want to blame the media, but a lot of the problem is with our own brains. As media consumers, there are a whole bunch of ways in which we love to be fooled, especially if we have to make a difficult decision about something. Scientific research shows that the human mind comes equipped with trapdoors that lead us to make stupid decisions not just about what we are going to do next, but also about the people and things around us.

The good news is, you can wake up and do something about it.

Propaganda: The Fake News Industry

There is something about our digital media that breeds manufactured news articles faster than newspapers printed on dead trees ever could, and that thing is online advertising. The giant media corporations Google and Facebook have created their own advertising systems that drop blocks of ads onto webpages that contract with them, then pay the owners of those pages money based on how many "clicks" the websites get from readers.

Are you following me? That means the more outrageous the news is, the more readers are driven to the fake news pages, and the page owners make more money. The higher the bullshit rises, so do the stacks of cash. Facebook and Google say they are trying out ways to pull the plug on fake news profit by making it possible for readers to flag fake stories. But the corporations say they can't stop it completely.

Meanwhile, the array of fake news stories has literally triggered panic around the world, like the social media reports of immigration checkpoints on street corners in Los Angeles, and a coup d'état in Mexico City over gas price protests. All bullshit.

In the 21st century, social media posts seem to play to our worst selves—thinking we know more than we do, lashing out without the real facts. But we are better than that. Knowing that there are patterns in how wrong information gets out into the public—and how we absorb it—makes it worth spending the time to understand how it all works.

Types of Fake News

- Completely fabricated reports, in which the whole story is made up ("Woman arrested for defecating on boss' desk after winning lottery" was a big one)

- Propaganda, which is completely or partially made-up information created to destroy a person or a group, starting with their credibility (like the one claiming President Barack Obama was not really a U.S. citizen)

- Biased news, which is often factual information, but packaged with a slant to politically influence the people who take it in (when white mass shooters in the U.S. are described as "mentally ill" but Black or Muslim mass shooters are "terrorists")

- Pseudo-events, which are publicity stunts to draw public attention, especially as a marketing ploy for a product brand (like when Red Bull, the energy drink, paid a skydiver to jump out of a balloon at the edge of space)

- Satire, which is the artistic use of comedy, ridicule, mockery, and caricature to deliberately attack the powerful or famous (like when The Onion writes a joke story about a government that turns out the next day to be true)

What is "Truth"?

What is "truth?" The Oxford English Dictionary defines it as "The quality or state of being true, i.e., 'he had to accept the truth of her accusation;'" also:

"'That which is true or in accordance with fact or reality, 'tell me the truth,' i.e., 'she found out the truth about him'"; and

"A fact or belief that is accepted as true, 'the emergence of scientific truths,' i.e., the fundamental truths about mankind.'"

Comedian Stephen Colbert uses the word "truthiness" to describe something that may or may not be true, but "feels like it." The English Oxford Dictionary has started including the term "post-truth," which means a situation in which facts matter less than an appeal to emotion.

For the most part, we define "truth" as a piece of information we can verify in some way; in journalism school, there will be at least one professor who insists that you're supposed to have three sources of information to back up every fact in a story.

With the ideas of "storytelling" and "truth," there has always been a fight between telling the story effectively and sticking to what can be backed up by two sources of information. We're talking about this more in our "Fact-Checking" chapter; you will come up with your own process for that, which fits in with your overall mission and vision. Do not skip this step.

As a journalist, whether you trust your sources or not, it's your job to find trustworthy information for your audience—not to manipulate what they think, but rather to educate people on what they need to know to make their lives better today. The best way to do that is to look at information in terms of where it is coming from. Naming the source for a piece of information is called "attribution," and it is absolutely crucial in any reporting you do. Many times, your audience cannot judge for themselves what is "true" if they do not know what your source of information is. There's a lot of fake news, but—big picture—the most dangerous tends to affect political systems.

Mental Trapdoors

Over the past few decades, a new line of research psychology has emerged around decision-making because of what are called cognitive biases and heuristics; to me, it's easier to think of them as common, predictable errors in human judgement—good old-fashioned brain farts. Understanding how cognitive biases—brain farts—work can be helpful in understanding why our media and political systems today are so screwy. As certain powerful interests on the global scene have discovered a source of power and wealth in creating false news content that is piped through social media mega-platforms, there emerges in the media landscape a driving need for accurate information to help everyday people live our lives.

Scientists have spent a lot of time studying brain farts and exactly how they work. Bottom line: Our brains are less like steel traps and more like slip-n-slides, because humans have varied and complicated ways of thinking.

Our cognitive biases are predictable, and they cause us to make mistakes, or wrong judgments. Once you start picking them up and looking at them, you realize a lot of these stupid moments come down to the things your grandma might have tried to teach you about when you were a kid. It's not brain surgery.

For many generations, economists have based their theories of how the world works on the assumption that people are reasonable and act in their own best interest. But anybody with a gambling uncle knows that's just not accurate; we make mistakes in judgment every day.

Since the 1960s, scientists who study decision-making have broken down the ways that our brains try to take shortcuts in logic.

We do it to make thinking easier, but in the process we make mistakes in judgment, and a lot of the time we don't want to correct them.

A lot of these mistakes in judgment have to do with our personal life experience and what is called the "subjective social reality" that comes from that: We all tend to judge everyone based on what we each individually understand, or think we understand. Subjective social reality is the gigantic door where racism and sexism and a horde of other kinds of discrimination storm into people's minds.

That means when you are a middle-class white male in a business suit running a television station, you may not relate to your coworker of color whose teenaged son just got frisked by the police; you may assume that he "did something wrong or he wouldn't have been stopped." Which would probably have been an incorrect assumption on your part, and you would have just missed the news story of the century, #BlackLivesMatter.

Heuristics: Brain Farts and How They Work

One of the words to describe these brain farts is "heuristics." Heuristics are shortcuts of logic that the mind uses to reach important decisions or judgments. The problem is, sometimes the "logic" isn't logical at all. Maybe if you're deciding on ice cream on a hot day, your normal processes can be fine. But what if you're getting ready to sift through a lot of charged information about a police shooting? Research shows that often your mind essentially substitutes a simpler question for whichever one you really face to make it easier for you—and in the process, your mind is opening itself up to bad decisions and bigoted reactions.

Those bigoted reactions come in the form of what are called "cognitive biases." These are types of faulty judgment that I think of as "predictable brain farts." These brain farts—there are dozens of identified and studied types—are separated into four categories:

- Problems from too much information ("TMI!") cause us to use weak judgment in deciding what's important, so we tend to: latch onto the first thing we see that fits what we already think; focus on what gets repeated often; pay attention to strange or surprising events rather than expected ones; notice when something has changed; distrust other people's judgment more than our own.

- Problems from a lack of meaning (like #AllLivesMatter misses the point of the #BlackLivesMatter movement) cause us to: imagine we see patterns in events when there is little information; fill in gaps of information using stereotypes and vague ideas; see in a more positive light anything that is more familiar to us; when gambling or calculating risk, we downplay probabilities, especially with numbers; imagine we can read others people's minds; and project what we know now on situations we encountered in the past or will encounter in the future.

- Problems from a need to act quickly (Be the first! Break the story!) can cause us to: adopt an attitude built on overconfidence; react to the most recent thing we're looking at rather than all the issues that might be looming; stick with projects we've been working on a long time, even though they may not be worth it; stick with the "status quo" to keep from making any mistakes; select simpler solutions over more complex ones, even though the complex one would better address the issue.

- And problems caused by the limits of memory ("I never said that!") include: we edit and build up some memories over others; we glom onto generalities instead of specifics; in our memory we boil down events to their most basic aspects; and we remember things differently based on how we experienced them.

To understand the full range of how our brains screw things up when we're trying to figure it all out, look for Buster Benson's "Cognitive Bias Cheat Sheet," which lays out the issues in an easy-to-read chart based on their cause; he maintains improved versions of it on his website, BusterBenson.com.

Breaking It Too Far Down

Underlying a lot of faulty judgment is our tendency for what is called attribute substitution. That means when we're given a question or issue that involves a lot of complicated thought, we tend to shy away from that question and gravitate towards a much simpler question that is completely different from the first one. (When Michael Brown was shot by a police officer in Ferguson, Missouri, headlines appeared in major media saying that he had robbed a local store rather than sticking to the known facts that he was unarmed and had been shot dead in the street by an officer. Two years later, "new video" was released that "cast doubt" on the original accusations Brown had robbed a store before his shooting. Brown's "crime" never happened, but some media outlets couldn't stop covering it.)

EXERCISES TO AVOID FAKE NEWS

- Find out where the original information came from—if anywhere at all?
- Conduct an Internet five-point search to find out more about a subject quickly, including sussing out sources of information, such as in the next step:
- Examine the websites where you found this information. Check to make sure there are actually names and dates on the stories. Check for unusual web addresses, including any that end in the letters "lo" or "co"—funky URLs sometimes hide fake news sites.
- Finally, check your own cognitive biases and make sure you are not just accepting a source because "it sounds good," or, on the other hand, rejecting one because its analysis is hard to hear.

CHECK IT OUT!

Buster Benson's breakdown of cognitive biases is a great thumbnail layout of the trapdoors in how we all think. It was created for use by decision-makers across a variety of industries, but really anyone can benefit from being reminded about the patterns in our own faulty thinking. It is huge, broken down into lists of the most common logical traps we all tend to face when we're making decisions. In a nutshell, Benson, an expert in systems analysis who's worked at Twitter and Slack, writes, "Thinking is hard because of 4 universal conundrums." He says all biases come from these four unsolvable problems or riddles: "there's too much information;" "there's not enough meaning;" "there's not enough time & resources;" and "there's not enough memory."

Each of these conundrums touches off a cascade of bad reasoning. For example, when there's too much information for us to take in, we tend to focus on what seems odd or threatening or surprising; when there's not enough meaning, we tend to fill in the gaps of our understanding with generalities; when there's not enough time or resources, we rush to assume that our quick take is "right" without deeper introspection; and when there's not enough memory, we cut back on what we need to remember by recycling the same small handful of memories over and over—among many other things.

Graphic designer John Manoogian III turned the whole list of 200-plus documented cognitive biases into an easy-to-read poster called the Cognitive Bias Codex, which you can check out online for free.

TECHNIQUE

Wake Up

I am suggesting you take steps to control your own perception of reality before you even set out to present it to the rest of the world. Start out by being aware of your own bubble and taking stock of how separate your experience is from others.

Using your own vision of yourself and the voice you want to project into the world, calibrate your take on the issues. Challenge yourself to find the viewpoint of another person who is not being heard within your story and dig out their perspective—whether you report on it or not. Do this systematically, every time.

TECHNIQUE

Who Can You Record?

Are there limits to who and what you can record with your phone or camera? The answer is yes, but the laws vary depending on where you live.

- In the U.S., the federal government allows a conversation to be recorded if one person in it gives consent—yes, that could be you.

- But some states require all parties to agree that recording is OK. So you have to go online and look that up for yourself.

- Most of the time though, as a community journalist, you are not only getting your subjects to agree to be recorded, but you might also be encouraging them to post and repost the recording.

- Recording children at any time requires some level of permission from the parents or institutions. Check online for paper forms you can download for this called "release forms." This is very important; don't skip this step.

- If you are a reporter for a radio or television station that is not allowed to air obscenities, pay attention to your recordings and make sure to keep forbidden words out.

STORY IDEA

As-It-Happens

One of the most creative approaches to information gathering is to set yourself the task of going through something and reporting about it as it unfolds—whether that happens live or is pre-recorded. In other words, you are setting out an epic experience for yourself or following someone else's, then recording or writing about every step of the way in following that experience. You could blend this personal experience with extensive book research if you want to. This is called "experiential"—it's based on your experience— and it can be extra compelling because it brings the everyday reader or listener or viewer right into the story as it unfolds.

   With this kind of approach, you as a journalist are documenting the sounds in the background, the voices of people who are there, aspects of this scene that may not themselves feel like they have anything to do with what's going on. But the idea is you're using the senses of the body to bring your audience to the scene of the story with you.

CHAPTER 4

INFORMATION GATHERING

"The media is absolutely essential to the functioning of a democracy. It's not our job to cozy up to power. We're supposed to be the check and balance on government."

—Amy Goodman, *Democracy Now!*

N ow, let's talk about how to go out and get the information you want to include. In this chapter, you will learn about how to ask questions, how to define information, how to gather it, and where to store it.

YOU WILL LEARN:

- Information only comes in six flavors: who, what, when, where, how and why.
- For the sake of interesting stories, it's never a bad idea to brainstorm as many points of information as you can, especially surprising and fun ones.
- Documents tell the story.
- Just because a certain kind of story has been done a million times doesn't mean it's not worth doing again.
- Label the names of each of your media pieces so that they are easier to organize over a long period of time; use the Kitty Litter Theory of news organization.

Deciding to take on a journalistic project is a big deal. But in a way, it's also very simple. That's because no matter what kind of reporting you do, information only comes in six flavors: who, what, when, where, how and why. When it comes time to start gathering information, these are the only questions your entire effort is ever built on. You use these words to dig, dig, and dig some more.

Information gathering is like gardening. You decide where the situation needs attention, grab a great big shovel, and start digging up the roots of what's there. Over time you might pull it out completely. If your reporting project gets big and complicated—which isn't that unusual—you might dig up this and dig up that and try to make sense out of it until there's literally dirt everywhere.

For that reason – to make things easier for yourself down the line—it's better to start your research in an organized manner, with timelines and outlines and even, maybe, spreadsheets.

To me, it is useful to think of a story in the voices of the people who lived it. So, I like to list people that I might interview; I actually make a document and write people's names and contact info on it. Then within that list, I jot down at least three questions for each of those people. Sometimes I voice-memo them on my phone. If I don't write them down or record them, I lose all my ideas; that's why I insist on some kind of system for storing them up.

Writing Good Questions

How do you ask the best questions to get the information you want? We already mentioned that your only choices are some combination of who, what, when, where, how, and why. But that still gives you a lot of leeway in deciding what you want to talk with people about.

As you think about the story that you're building, there will always be many ways to tell it. If you can figure out early on the big fact you are looking at and the burning questions that come from it, you'll have a focus on the information you are looking for. Then, if big surprises are unleashed by your research, you will be ready.

In terms of what information you should gather, by and large you will always want:

- The history of your subject: who runs it, who started it, what it's for
- Why it is important
- How much it costs and who pays for it
- Where it takes place
- What is in the near future for this thing

"Get it On 'Paper!'"

Here's another super important thing: Documents tell the story. Where there is no documentation in writing, audio, or videotape, there is no story. Listen to the person, but then hunt down the documents. Anything that's written down can be a source of information, from government notices to lawsuits and social media posts. Emails and text messages of government employees and elected officials on the clock also count under Freedom of Information Act rules—look for more on these items in the upcoming chapter "What Is Investigative Reporting?"

Gather, gather, gather—but don't forget about storage. For the sake of interesting stories, it's never a bad idea to brainstorm as many points of information as you can, especially surprising and fun ones. But whatever information you collect, you need to store it where you can easily grab it. That means keeping links on a spreadsheet, or crayon pictures in a storyline, or ballpoint pen on cookie wrappers in a shoebox—something.

Digital Tupperware?

But don't stop there: If this is going to be a project with a bunch of thoughts and interviews and links to articles and images, you need to think in advance how you are going to store that information so you can get to it when you need it. I want to apologize in advance because I am a broken record on this.

You're going to build a digital home entertainment center with shelves and nooks to hold your media where everyone can see it—we'll talk about what that means later. But holding on to your digital materials over time is a real issue you should think about from the start.

Labels Are Your Friend

You are finding a mountain of fascinating stuff for your exposé about Amazon's expedited shipping policy. You've got articles and video and testimonies and legal documents. What do you do with it all? You should plan to label each of these items—whether it's a Word doc or an MP3 or something from the future that hasn't been invented yet—using three words or less, to make your whole process easier (and make one of those "words" a date, to help you track these things over longer periods of time).

This is the Kitty Litter Theory of news organization—clump your shit together every chance you get:

- All file labels with the same first word will clump together within any folder; you can add numbers to those files to control the order you see them in. The point is you should be able to open a folder and know exactly what each of these items are and where they go.
- Choose one overall name for your project.

Mine for this book was CITJO. Then I had ten sub-files named for each chapter: interviewing, fact_checking, processing, you get the idea. In the files, I saved downloads of articles backgrounding that chapter, and these pieces were named things like CITJO_interviewing_ hostileinterviews, and CITJO_processing_martiniglass.

Even now, when I click on the folder, the research pieces all line up in order—I can find everything without a sweat. I can tell what each piece is about and where it goes just by looking at the label. That way, if I ever have to upload that file to something? I can know what it is just by looking at the label.

Special note: These boring random tips about documents and labeling will save you hours of grief. Hours.

What is "Information?"

It might seem ridiculous, but not all information is created equal. As we have mentioned repeatedly, who, what, when, where, how, and why are the building blocks of all information. But what about situations where you are trying to gather information about, for example, a law enforcement situation? Anything written in a police report is widely considered to be fact. However, anything said by a defendant—the person charged with a crime—outside the courtroom is not. Anything written or described within the pages of a tort claim—a kind of legal "fuck you" notice someone writes to a government agency to let it know the details of how they're going to sue that agency—becomes information that you can write about or broadcast within a story, even though it may not have yet been proven in court. You can't present all the information as true, but you can report that they are charges in a tort claim.

Once a lawsuit is resolved, most of the time the winner's account of events is considered to be "true." That becomes an issue when, as happens a lot of times, legal settlements are "sealed," meaning if the two parties resolved their beef out of court with some kind of cash payout, they can all agree to keep it secret. Unfair criminal charges against juveniles of color often end this way—one of the things that make it hard for newsrooms to track racial profiling. By and large, as you move forward in your career as a street journalist, you'll find that documents tell the story. Don't take anybody's word for it; demand to see something in writing or on tape to back up what anyone's telling you, then use your toolbox to suss out the backup.

But just the same, I have gotten a lot of stories because of my good relationships with people who work in bureaucracies, and also from consumers ripped off by the retail system. Where my modest newspaper could not afford to file thousand-dollar Freedom of Information Act requests, people by the dozens came to us seeking an advocate in a wide range of civil rights conflicts. Many times, these people would bring in big stacks of their own documents detailing their legal battles or bureaucratic problems.

Keep an Open Door, and Be Careful

In all my years of experience as a community reporter, the most important source of information I ever had was people who walked into my office. No matter how complicated the online world gets, that one thing hasn't changed. The more difficult aspect of this is gaining the public trust. One family who came to my newspaper had a son in mental health crisis in the juvenile jail; the parents argued in front of me over whether their child would be injured by jail staff if they talked to a member of the media. Whatever you do, as a blogger or podcaster or video broadcaster, never forget to treat people fairly and give them a right to privacy. There is a big difference between public figures and everyday people. If you use your digital platforms to invade the privacy of innocent people, you could damage lives in ways that will take years to overcome.

Finding Information in Bulk

Here I'm going back to the information factory. The news staff goes out into the community and gathers information; then we bring it into the newsroom to organize it and then make it available to the public in bite-sized chunks so it's easy to chew. When you look at it that way, you realize almost anyplace can be a source of information that might help your listeners and viewers and readers every single day.

One important place to check for information as you're thinking about stories are the websites of local government officials. City council and county supervisor agendas can be interesting to read because so much of our lives are impacted by them and we don't realize it. Here are a couple quick tips on learning the ropes of local governments:

- As you scrutinize what's on a city council or county commission agenda, keep in mind that sometimes the most boring things are the most important things.
- Generally speaking, people want to know how their taxpayer dollars are spent. That's probably why "follow the money" is one of the most famous sayings in journalism. For that reason, if you're researching items on an agenda, look for anything on there with a monetary value. Which is the most expensive item you can find? I spent many years reporting from City Hall, and one of the things I learned is that, by and large, the more paid staff there are attached to an agenda item, the more taxpayer money that item costs. Which agenda item includes the most

people from different government bureaus all working together on the same thing, and how many are there?

- And lastly, which agenda items are being brought by actual residents? Speaking of "brought by the residents:" Using the Internet, in two minutes or less, can you find out which city bureau is the most often sued?

Check Ratings Websites

When I look at the subject matter of a given story, I think about what sources of information are considered to be the most important for that particular field.

For example, once I covered a story about a civil rights lawsuit against a restaurant, and one source I used was Yelp, the online retail rating system. The story was about a suit brought by an African-American diner against the restaurant, which she said denied her service because of her race. On Yelp I was able to see that a second diner of color had been refused service at that same restaurant on the same evening. Unfortunately for the story, when I emailed the second diner using the Yelp email system, it took him about four months to respond—long after the situation had been resolved. So, heads up on that.

Another time, in my town, a family of violent gang members used a beloved community restaurant where the longtime owner had retired to a different state as a front for their drug dealing. By the time they were taken into custody, that restaurant's Yelp page had been speculating for two years that the place was a front for drug dealing. It made for a pretty fascinating read, by the way.

Friends and Sources

If you dream of building a media outlet, no matter how modest, you need to start from the beginning to bring other people into what you are doing—who you ask advice from; who helps you set up your website; who takes pictures; who gives you tips on what you should write about. This is the start of building community around your media outlet.

You might think that as a journalist you should be independent of all institutions within your zone. But you can't do your job without building relationships with the people who matter within your community of coverage. That does not necessarily mean just the bigwigs—I mean the everyday people. It's their lives you are working to uplift as a street journalist. They are your readers, your neighbors, the people shopping at your local grocery store. These are people who are out there doing their jobs, the people who are likely to be sources for your reporting. They may not all have voted for the same president, but everyone is a pillar of your community—not the bigwigs, the everyday people.

And as you create your street journalism media platform, look around for community institutions—businesses and nonprofit organizations—to make friends with people who support your work. That means approaching small institutions as well as individuals and asking what they think the important stories are. That's part of the actual purpose of a media outlet.

I bring this up because in journalism school you are taught, as reporter, not to have a relationship with the people you are reporting about. You are supposed to be "objective"—you're not supposed to have an opinion about it. But in real life, communities are made up of people with common connections and goals. Be aware of these connections and be intentional about who you connect with; make sure your connections reflect your mission and vision as a journalist.

Building Blocks of Community: Kids

When you are making your big plans, you are smart to lay out a special table for kids. Kids are the secret sauce of community building, one way or another; if journalism is like a garden, kids are the blossoms of the coming season. In the old days of newspapers, one of the things that made a person want to pick one up was all the pictures of their family members inside—mostly kids. When people could see their families reflected in the paper, it gave them a sense of ownership over not just that media outlet but their own town.

It's strange to think of it now, but for many generations in the 20th century it was kids who actually delivered the local newspapers. Thousands of kids, across the country, for many, many years, were part of the newspaper economy. One of the biggest labor strikes in U.S. history pitted the children who sold newspapers in New York City against the most powerful newspapermen around, Joseph Pulitzer and William Randolph Hearst, in 1899.

When you consider that your ability to stay alive as a media outlet depends on having relationships with all the people who eat up your stories in one way or another, building community partnerships is one of the most important things that can keep you going.

Consider all of the different ways that you can have contact with your potential audience. At the humble community radio station where I work, we tend to connect to our audience via, number one, the airwaves; number two, the Internet—our website; number three, email bulletins; and number four, tables with volunteers offering information live at community events. Consider casting a wide net to build community around your work.

In that way, I think the more our tools change, the more they stay the same. And the same tendency of wanting to see ourselves reflected in a platform plays out today with the people that make reader comments on your blog, YouTube channel, Periscope, or any of the other infinite platforms out there.

Partnerships: Using Touchstones

Because I am a middle-aged white woman, when I first started working in the African American media, I established for myself a handful of people that I thought of as touchstones. In some cases, because I have had to cover other peoples' communities as a journalist, I have needed more knowledgeable voices than my own— that is, people I could go to who are experts in their communities. Reaching out for connections who can help you understand issues is one way to bring equity into play. I have four touchstones in my life at any one time, so I recommend more good advice rather than less good advice on that.

The second way of taking advantage of partnerships is through working with organizations. Sometimes, understanding the message that an organization offers can help you learn about other things too, like how the political system works and how to follow the money it runs on. That can be true no matter what side of the political equation the group is on. In my community radio newsroom, we make time every single week for multiple live interviews with nonprofits doing social change work on the grassroots level. Their staff and volunteers are usually everyday people trying to use their free time for something constructive. When you hear about the grassroots organizations are doing all the time—things you have not been reading about in the newspapers or seeing on television—you can find all sorts of worthy story ideas.

Bringing It Together

Just because a certain kind of story has been done a million times doesn't mean it's not worth doing again. That's especially true in cases that are important to consumers. Where I live in the state of Oregon, one local radio station used to walk through the Made in Oregon store every holiday season and photograph all the tags that indicated the item was made in a third world sweat shop. Another common story is a look through your county health department restaurant and café inspection records to see if there were any spectacular failures recently; in some counties, the health inspector reports are available online in easy-to-use widgets. Another evergreen reporting project involves looking at state dam inspection records; in some states, a majority of the dams have not been inspected for many, many years. When one of these dams collapses it can wipe out whole towns.

No matter what kind of project you have going, the single most important skill you could ever put to use is curiosity. Some people are natural seekers, and those people keep digging until they find what they're looking for—it could be a Victorian recipe for lemon cookies, or an NSA document disclosed through WikiLeaks. You keep digging and digging until you have big piles of information. Then, suddenly, you're drowning in information.

Talk to People!

Using online resources does not take away from the need to speak to real people for any given story. You should always be speaking with real people and not just relying on the Internet, if at all possible. That is because the Internet creates problems of its own, especially with veracity.

On the other hand, in my newsroom we have had a standing rule that every name is run through a search engine. If it's a subject of great interest, go back as far as three or four pages in search results, if possible. That's always keeping in mind that whatever comes up in the searches may or may not be accurate. You are examining each piece for a sense of context on where its information is coming from, a look at the bubble around that information including which community the information was aimed at and anything else of interest—keeping in mind the information may or may not be accurate.

Not only do you need to learn how to verify information you get from the Internet, you also need to learn how to suss out the bad information. We'll talk about fact-checking in a later chapter.

EXERCISES

- Go online to any government website. Find the webpage describing meeting agendas. Always in scrutinizing government, you are looking for contradictions or red flag issues that might impact the public. Oftentimes, financial impacts hit everyday people hard; other times it might be a lack of vision for needed services. Is there a specific issue that you see your community struggling through right now? Look at the agenda for the upcoming meeting. Is there any item that impacts the issue you have identified as crucial, and are there any services earmarked for that issue? Try a different strategy: Identify what looks to be the most boring item on the agenda. See if you can discover how much money is linked to that particular item, and what exactly is that money to be spent on.

- Go online to your local county government website and look for the health department. See if they make available any kind of database of health department inspections of local restaurants. See if you can find the local health department inspection of your favorite restaurant and see what score it got.

- Go to one of your local government websites. See if there is an auditor's bureau; an auditor is an official who investigates whether their own government agencies are doing a good job. Look and see if the auditor has issued any recent reports. If so, now check the webpage of the bureau or department the auditor was examining. See if you can find a response from them to the auditor's report.

CHECK IT OUT!

Fake news is ancient; in fact, you could say it is the only news we had before the 20th century. Starting almost one thousand years ago, "blood libel" stories repeated around the world spread lies specifically saying that Jews drank the blood of Christian children during the annual Jewish liberation festival called Passover. All throughout history, the telling and retelling of these lies has inflamed everyday people into mob murders of Jewish men, women, and children.

In the early 20th century, newspaper publisher Randolph Hearst became famous for "yellow journalism," which in part established the lasting tradition of violent and "truthy" reporting in newspapers. When the U.S. invaded the island nation of Cuba in 1895, Hearst set out to make money on bloody, violent accounts of the action, and he did.

TECHNIQUE

How to Take Notes

Once you decide to jump into a story, you realize you need to be able to take notes. People are not born knowing how to do this. Check out these tips on note-taking:

- If you take a few moments to prepare for your interview or press conference, this will help your note-taking in a big way. Note down in advance the names of people talking, names of reports or anything you know they will be talking about, and you'll follow their comments more easily in the moment.

- Start out by heading your note-taking document with the date and names of important people on the scene with you.

- Move on by writing down the most important information you can find from whatever it is you are reporting on.

- For some kinds of reporting, this includes the sounds you are hearing, the smells you are smelling, all of the senses—be sure to check in with them.

- When you are done, go back and read over your notes as soon as possible—but no more than two hours of first writing them down—and fill in all the holes you can. Try to remember everything you missed writing down.

STORY IDEA

Describing the System

One of the most important areas lacking consistent media coverage is how criminal justice systems really work. We see videos of street violence all the time, but courtrooms and jails (where a lot of mentally ill people are housed) operate outside the limelight much of the time. There's a lot going on there: prison labor systems, sexual violence, white supremacist recruitment, racial harassment, drug smuggling—your local jail is a story in itself.

Taking your cue from reporting on police shootings, obtaining rare videos from inside institutions could be key tools for a story about that. YouTube is a hotspot for info like this; jail video is a category you could start with. It can be hard to find verifiable information about what goes on in lockdown, but another great source of rare public information on jail conditions is lawsuits filed against prison and jail systems. These are published on computer systems you can read at your county or state courthouse.

Get ready to take lots of notes; if you can plan to attend an actual trial and cover its resolution, you could be writing a dozen stories or more.

CHAPTER 5

INTERVIEWING TIPS

One of the things that can make or break a great story is the ability to bring in the voices of other people, not just your own. Sometimes the whole point of a story is to focus on one interesting or influential person, because something about their life inspires and fascinates others. The goal of this chapter is to outline the basic techniques of interviewing, different types of interviews, and offer a couple of tips to help make your interviews successful.

YOU WILL LEARN:

- How to unlock people so they'll open up and tell their story
- How to ask short questions and shut up while your subject talks
- How to speak to people with respect, no matter who they are
- For people from the dominant paradigm interviewing someone who does not look like them—such as someone white who is interviewing a person of color—how to build a respectful connection with your subject

When it comes to street journalism, interviewing skills are a superpower, like flying or laser beam eyes. The ability to lead an organized, intelligent interview can elevate any project or broadcast, no matter what the subject is. Not only do audiences consistently show up anywhere for interviews with elected officials and politicians, we also love interviews with everyday people on the street. We love to find out what makes people tick.

Though a lot of interviews you see or hear in the media seem to happen on the spur of the moment, many—if not most— are tightly organized, with all the questions written out in advance.

As a street journalist, approaching an important interview, I would strongly suggest you do the same—prepare yourself with questions written out in advance.

You can always choose not to use a single solitary one of your questions, but it never hurts to have the basic information spelled out in front of you—whether on paper or a smartphone including the basic facts of an event that you will be talking about and the web address for people who want more information.

The key to opening up the person you're interviewing is to find the right question or a comment that gives them the sense that they can trust you. Getting basic information right in advance, such as how to say their name and details on what they're there to talk about, can go a long way.

Shut Up and Listen

The First Law of Interviewing is: Ask your question, then shut up and listen. Stop yourself from "listening out loud"—saying "huh!" or "yes, that's right!" to everything your guest says. Let them talk without your voice coming over the microphone at all unless you have something important to say. Adopting this habit can take you far in journalism, especially in any kind of broadcast. For street journalists, nothing kills an interview more dead than airspace taken up mostly by the interviewer's voice.

Do It with Respect

Everybody in the world has their own story. Some might seem more interesting than others, but almost anything can be interesting depending on how it's framed. That's why it's important to speak to people with respect, no matter who they are. That means if you're interviewing someone who does not have a place to live, or if you are interviewing a police officer, or a member of the city council, a business owner, a child, you will always make it a point to speak with respect.

Even if all the other people around you are not speaking with respect, you still will speak with respect. As a journalist, best is when you feel comfortable asking almost anything, when you are able to comfortably chat with people and slowly, systematically, pull out their own individual story, whatever it may be.

Picking the Locks

I think people are like locked boxes. As an interviewer, you are trying to pick the lock on whoever you're speaking to, getting them to open up and tell their story, whatever it is. The full-frontal assault-style interview where the guest is blindsided by hostile questions is a format you have seen before. But if you want to get the best possible interview, you need to show respect to the person you're speaking to and gain their trust. To me, it does not matter if you are interviewing the president of the police officers' union, or houseless family, or a community organizer, or a member of the city council.

As a journalist, you should treat everybody as people first.

I used to be intimidated by elected officials and bigwigs. Now I find that just treating everyone with equal courtesy no matter the situation is actually the shortcut to an effective interview and words in the can.

Equity Matters

For many years, I have worked as a white reporter in an African-American community. Many times, I have had to prove myself trustworthy to people in a difficult situation. One of the most important suggestions I can make to people interviewing someone who does not look like them—especially someone white who is interviewing a person of color—is to just stop talking so much.

In my situation, I see that so many of the hurtful and tiresome comments that make people uncomfortable around each other—especially people of color uncomfortable around white people—are almost all the small comments about unimportant things. Little jokes, words spoken under the breath, a long rambling travel story about how someone found spirituality in India after eating the food. As a white person, I try to be vigilant about what I say and do, but I'm constantly learning lessons about the world around myself too.

Be Able to Shift in the Moment

The most important thing to know about your big reporting project is that whatever is meant to happen, happens. Get a handle on errors and ethics, but also be prepared to shift your approach if something happens. That's because something is probably going to happen.

Once I worked with a crew in a small nonprofit newsroom to put out an investigative report about military contracts in the state of Oregon. It was a crew of about eight volunteer journalists working on this hard-hitting issue, but the one reporter who was supposed to interview the industry guys was completely intoxicated on cannabis when she recorded her report. I never recommend this, by the way, but it's what happened.

This volunteer reporter attended the first ever business fair our state had ever held for local companies hoping to win a U.S. Department of Defense (some people call it the "Department of War") contract for some product that they produce. In this case the reporter took a recorder into the convention center and started asking questions of the people behind the tables in the hallways. One company made beanbag chairs that they thought should be inset into all of the upholstery in Stryker brigade attack tanks; our reporter laughed and said on the recording, "That is sooooo '70s!"— an almost-polite way of asking "why do tanks need beanbag chairs?"

Then she approached a man standing at a table that announced it was the Native American Defense Contractors' Association. "You don't look Native American," she giggled. He said, "Well, we're working hard at outreach . . . " This volunteer was just stoned enough to ask the most awkward questions. As I checked off from my list each assignment from the reporters who put them together, they seemed completely scattered; for a minute I panicked.

But each piece was solid and rooted in its subject matter. In fact, the stoned reporter asked the exact right harsh questions in a uniquely nonthreatening way that drew unguarded answers from her subjects; her work was the highlight of the entire report. All the pieces fell right into place. This is all just to say—sometimes, be ready to change your plans.

Talk to Everyday People

As a journalist, you're always talking to somebody. But it is important to remember the difference between public officials and everyday people. If you find yourself in the situation where you're interviewing everyday people—that is, people who are not subject to public attention on a regular basis—it can be difficult to get people to comment on the questions you're trying to ask. Again, it's about trust; most people do not trust the media in general. But building trust with your fellow human beings is at the very heart of journalism; as a reporter, your job is to draw out the truth in people and events, and the best way to do that is through relationships. At the end of the day, most people just really do not want to be surprised. You can let your reporting subjects know what to expect from your reporting without giving them veto power over your work. In my experience, the best way to gain people's trust in the moment is to number one, specifically describe what it is I want from them; number two, let them know what that involves; number three, if they agreed to do these things, then I repeat them like a laundry list as we go through the steps. Walk folks through it and help them understand their own power in your local community, and you will build bridges that will take you places in your reporting for years to come.

Interviewing a Group

Much of the time we are doing an interview, we are one on one, talking to one person at a time. If you are in a situation where you are interviewing a group of people, heads up. It's hard to take written notes in that kind of scenario, and if you're making an audio recording of the group interview, it can be difficult to track who said what later on.

Having said that, dynamic group discussions can be some of the funniest things to listen to as you're driving down the road or moving quickly on a bicycle. Recordings of dynamic group discussions about interesting topics—whether they are audio discussions or videotape discussions—can be fun ways to share ideas with family and friends.

So, the most important thing to remember if you are preparing an interview with a group of people is to draw up a list of simple questions in advance. Then go ahead and sketch out two complex questions that you could pull out at the opportune moment. It's worth it to write down a schedule of who speaks and when—that's called a run sheet—so you can realistically track how you're spending time in the moment. And find ways to restate who is speaking as the interview progresses.

"Breaking News" Interviews

Sometimes there's been a big fire, or a shooting, or some other unusual event that calls for extraordinary reporting measures. If you get called out to find out what's going on during a big public emergency, find out before you go who the spokesperson is for the government bureau or department that takes care of that sort of emergency; it should be on the Internet.

There are public service websites that distribute this information especially for purposes of public safety. Go online and search "press releases, city, police, fire." You might do a web search for "flash alert system" or something of that nature before it's time to go cover an emergency and see if you can hook up two sources of information in advance. This could save you hours of digging around for information.

Making Contacts

If you are organized enough to establish yourself as a regular reporter in one of these emergency areas, you should consider exchanging cell phone information with the spokesperson in charge of that area. Many journalists also listen to the police scanners covering their neighborhoods; you can find them with a quick search online.

But here is an important point: Sometimes journalists can get emotionally carried away in the moment. Sometimes we get arrogant and demanding, even occasionally threatening. When it comes to powerful people and you, the truth is that they have a job to do, and you have a job to do. Think in advance about always remaining respectful of the people you interview, whether you personally like them or not. Even if you think that person is the worst human on Earth, find a way to be respectful of them, because relationships are at the heart of your job, and if that official is in charge today, he or she will be in charge the next time too. Get ready to create positive relationships with people you disagree with; it's not a bad thing.

Above all, never act in such a way as to endanger the electronic equipment of your employer that you may have with you at a breaking news event. If you lose your cool and aggressively call out, for example, the government official in front of you, you will be cut off and thrown out of the scene so fast your head will spin. In fact, never be rude to any kind of emergency official at the scene of a breaking news event, Got it? You laugh now, but this has happened; don't let it happen to you.

Crisis Interviews

As we talk about best practices for a news interview, there are times when the situation takes you beyond a simple setting of asking someone basic questions.

For me, that moment came one night when a teenage boy's mother and his father knocked at the office door just as I was locking up the office. When they came in and we sat at the conference room table, they could not agree on whether they should be talking to me or not. I assured them that I would not publish anything without their knowledge and that I would have to check with them on any information I did uncover through any investigation that I would do.

I was able to earn their trust. The events of their story, covered in a state police investigation that ran to more than a thousand pages, are worthy of a documentary film. Suffice it to say we were able to get their son out of a juvenile jail for several months while he recovered from a mental health breakdown. Then he had to go back inside, if you can imagine that.

Sometimes interviews can actually have life or death stakes. It's my personal view as a journalist that I never want to harm any of the people I'm encountering in my work who are already victims and already coming from a place of vulnerability and pain, of this nature especially.

Hostile Interviews

Sometimes you have to interview someone who does not want to be interviewed. Most often, this is some sort of public official, but sometimes it can be someone from the private sector, like a business owner or attorney.

The best way to tackle this kind of situation is to have the questions written out that you want answered and to maintain a civil voice, whatever that looks like. Even if the questions that you have to ask are really harsh, the best chance you have of getting an actual answer from the person you're talking to is to maintain your cool.

Most hostile interviews happen in person—whether it's on the phone, in a press conference, or in a public place such as a courthouse or City Hall. That's because when you're trying to text or email someone who does not want to talk to you, it's easy for them to just not reply.

Sometimes in hostile interviews, it can be possible to turn the emotional dynamic around and reap some interesting nuggets of insight. Even in really tough interviews, when you have to ask the mayor directly if he lied to the people, it is still possible to have a productive or even positive relationship with the person you're interviewing. The key is to establish a sense of respect for your interview subject; if you want a deep and honest response to your tough questions, you must establish some kind of bridge to connect you to your subject.

A great example of this principle in action was law enforcement using attack dogs on nonviolent demonstrators, as happened in 2016 and 2017 in North Dakota at the Standing Rock encampment to block construction of an oil pipeline under a tributary of the Missouri River.

With her crew filming dog attacks against the "water protectors," as the demonstrators were called, journalist Amy Goodman closely shouted questions at the dog handlers, calling out the blood on one dog's mouth. Goodman says on tape to the dog handler: "Ma'am, your dog just bit this protester. Your dog just bit that protester. Are you telling the dogs to bite the protesters?" The dog handler did not respond, but the exchange electrified watchers around the world.

Sometimes your subject is waiting and hoping for someone to ask them the hard questions and now there you are. Again, I find the most important thing is to keep a thread of collegiality with the person I am trying to interview. I personally feel that if I am unable to establish some degree of trust, then the interview is difficult to move forward with.

This is a pretty stark contrast with some of my colleagues, who feel that each interview should be, by definition, a hostile interview. I simply disagree with that approach.

Confrontational Interviews

Within the world of hostile interviews, there is a subset I think of as "confrontational." This means an interview in which you plan to get to go head to head against some kind of powerbroker—perhaps a corporate leader, an elected official, or government figure. The best way to do these types of interviews is by knowing the answers to the questions before you ask them. That is always difficult. But it's not impossible. Confrontational interviews allow you to tell a story about injustice and bring the injustice to a power broker within the establishment with the intention of shifting a situation. Once I did a series of articles about a tiny neighborhood in Portland that had never been hooked up to the city's electrical or sewage grid until 2013. Meanwhile, the homeowner's association management suddenly hit all the impoverished residents with the cost of water leaks going back 40 years. One homeowner in particular stood out because on top of being slapped with the new bill for past leaks, her water bill was hiked even higher after an incompetent plumbing repairman hired by the HOA managers damaged her pipes. I did two years of research, then brought my findings to city officials and confronted them on it; they allowed the homeowner a fast-tracked free attorney through Legal Aid to try to hold on to her house.

Deeper Interviews

When you are brainstorming the questions you are going to ask during your important interview, you might be wondering how you can dig into your subject's upbringing. After you spend a while asking the basic questions, you begin to yearn for something more.

One of my favorite surprise questions to ask people I interview is: Do you ever write? Almost everyone asked that question has answered with a fun story. Another good question is: Who is your most important inspiration? I also like: What was the turning point of your life? Give yourself permission to be creative. One question a former writing teacher of mine liked to ask was: If I told your mother when you were little that this is what you were going to do, what would she have said? I always loved that question. If you give it a little thought, you can come up with your own best questions.

If you are doing your interview on a broadcast medium with audio or video, consider including sounds and pictures of the environment as you go. Sometimes it can be possible that the environment itself is also a character in a story. That's especially true someplace where there is a steady noise such as at the ocean, or by a river or in the farm or a city. When you are doing storytelling style interviews using radio or video equipment, taking separate recordings of the surrounding noise without any voices can elevate the story itself by bringing the listener or the watcher right there to the scene. Again, don't forget to ask the person you're interviewing about strange senses, such as the sense of smell. Anything to get your guest to open up fun and even talkative stories and comments is what you're looking for.

Don't Be Co-opted

I am going to say something really controversial here: I don't believe rage has any place in the newsroom. When a reporter or a journalist is filled with rage it's the interview where it really comes out. There is such a thing as an abusive interview. I become deeply concerned every time I hear an interview of this nature.

To me, every time somebody puts out an abusive interview— with screaming voices, name-calling, and personal attacks—it's a betrayal of what we in community media should be all about, which is sharing each other's stories.

Venting your personal outrage is different—outrage leads people to calling up legislators. Here, I am more concerned with rage that leads people to swing baseball bats.

When we as journalists allow rage to shape our words, we are opening ourselves up to manipulation by others who have an axe to grind. We allow other people to use us as weapons against their enemies. It's better to maintain control of your own work and not allow yourself to be co-opted by others' rage, even if they are well-meaning. If you have to do the rage thing, take it to a blog and call it "opinion."

EXERCISES

- Choose one person you would love to interview. Write three quirky questions to ask that person. Also write three normal questions to ask that person.

- Brainstorm your own personal interviewing checklist. Make a list, like a laundry list, of questions you'd definitely want to make sure you always ask every time you interview anyone. Add five questions that are fun that you might rotate in and out of interviews. Consider including a standard intro and outro for yourself if your interviews are recorded for broadcast in some way.

- Brainstorm on a cocktail napkin, as they say, a five-part podcast, each one interviewing an expert on some topic of interest to you. Choose five expert areas, each one a podcast episode, and for each one post three questions you would have for the expert on that topic for that podcast.

CHECK IT OUT!

Probably no single incident represents the power of street journalism in the U.S. more than the police killing of Michael Brown in 2014; it was a spark that exploded the #BlackLivesMatter movement into the public eye along with the national police accountability movement. In August of 2014, when Brown was gunned down by the police in Ferguson, Missouri, a witness to the killing, Emanuel Freeman—also known as @TheePharoah— tweeted several pictures of the scene as it unfolded in real time. When the streets of Ferguson filled with protests, the independent media company This Week in Blackness responded with programming and live streams. With the hashtag #BlackLivesMatter, hundreds of people have stepped up to record and post cellphone video of police violence, including fatal shootings and altercations.

TECHNIQUE

A Prep List for Interviewing

- Be prepared. If at all possible, run everyone and everything through a search engine. Before you go.
- Make sure all of your electronics are charged well in advance; don't wait until you're facing someone across the table to realize that you cannot record the interview.
- Always show up with a handful of questions written down on something.
- Always show up with a sense of what you're doing there and why this interview/press conference is important. Especially if

it is important to you for different reasons than the person you're interviewing.

- If it is a personality profile, always ask the basic questions of where are you from, when were you born, where is your family now? Always ask people their official titles, and quadruple check the spelling of every name including location names. Police officers and sheriffs, like military people, have ranks—use them and don't get them wrong.

- As part of preparing for your interview, if it is an important story or a personality profile, spend a few minutes thinking about what makes this person tick. Write it down.

- If this is a super important interview—a chat with your favorite celebrity or author you may never meet again—try to think of a question that will surprise your guest. Not in a mean way but perhaps looking at social issues of interest to the wider public, relating to what you learned in researching their life.

- Never show hostility toward your guest. I can tell you from experience that it is unproductive and detrimental to your long-term goals. You can be firm, even blunt or maybe curt, but you lose control of the interview when you become insulting. Don't be that guy.

- You should never talk more than the person you're trying to interview—put your question out there, and then be quiet while your guest answers.

- At the same time, if you have a guest who is especially wordy and cannot control his or her desire to talk, there's a point where you have to gain control of the interview and cut off your guest. Be kind about it.

TECHNIQUE

Covering Protests

When it comes to breaking news, covering political protests is an advanced skill. These events can be filled with joy, or they might be dangerous to protesters and media alike. Take a moment to think about what you're going to do before running out to report on a political protest. Here are some things to keep in mind:

- Now more than ever, you need to make sure all your electronic devices are charged up, with spare energy items as well.

- Before you go, check the location of the protest. Ask yourself: Is it a march, or a rally? Is it in one place or is it moving around? Where will it start, and where is it likely to end? Note these things down on a device or on paper or something.

- Once on the scene, try to identify key people you might want to interview, such as organizers, city attorneys, or police officials; always look for the mayor. If you're not sure what they look like, do this research online before you go.

- If you are heading into a crowd of freaked out people, try to remain calm. Never shout at law enforcement, but if they are doing something that seems wrong, go ahead and question them about it to their faces (independent journalist Amy Goodman directly confronted attack dog handlers injuring indigenous people, who were blocking construction of an oil pipeline at Standing Rock, North Dakota, in 2016), but to keep confrontational situations from getting worse, you absolutely must remain calm.

- I strongly suggest using a buddy system when live streaming or recording street protests to keep the camera-person safe from car traffic and just falling over things. It works best with two people.

TECHNIQUE

Rediscovering History

When it comes to information gathering, the history of your issue is one of the most important things. But where do you find that? You should check digital sources, like media outlets. But above all, I want to suggest that you talk with old people. Find the ones who lived through whatever you're writing about in the past and ask them what happened. You might find these stories are different than the ones you pulled from the old newspapers and television reels. Remember how cognitive biases work, like the ones you read about in the "Fake News" chapter—so in deciding how you are going to investigate your story, keep in mind that you are liable to believe whichever source of information you took in first. Keep that in mind as you work through your story; calibrate, or change your approach if you need to.

STORY IDEA

Ask People about Places

Reporting about a place? If you don't know the complete history of wherever you're talking about, you can ask other people for that history in a way that adds a lot to your story. Find the characters who lived then. Start out by asking these sources general questions such as: What was this place like 100 years ago? Again, specifically ask about physical senses to get your listeners' or viewers' attention — imagine the smells, the sounds, the sights?

Start with the small details of daily lives, then pull back into a slightly bigger view of local city life. Then lastly, take a bigger look of who was president at the time, and what the economy was based on, and what impact that had on whatever subject you're looking at.

CHAPTER 6

WHAT IS INVESTIGATIVE REPORTING??

"When I first drove by it on the way to my uncle's house, it shocked me. It's desolate land. To me, it's very beautiful land. I'm from here. I'm very rooted here, and all of a sudden I see this 18-foot steel fence. It looked like a scar, like a cut that'd just been sutured."

—multimedia journalist Cecilia Balli describing the U.S.-Mexico border wall, which she depicted in photography, writing, and radio podcasting on PRI's *The World* in 2015

The goal of this chapter is to help define the term "investigative reporting," and to give you methods on how to plan and finish reporting projects that impact your issues.

YOU WILL LEARN:

- Often, what makes one story an investigative story and another story not is that an investigative project will explain how some important process works—or doesn't work—in your local community.

- The only motivation for investigating an organization or individual must be as part of a policy analysis and not for personal reasons.

- As a journalist, no matter what platform you use, you can establish your own important investigative reporting territory that you continue to cover over time.

- Wherever you go in the world of journalism, the documents tell the story.

This might sound silly, but it's not always easy to define the term "investigative reporting." That's part of the reason why we always see legal fistfights over whether the Freedom of Information Act—the national law controlling access to government records—was created for all residents, or just for "journalists." Smart reporters using public records requests to stop corruption in government—that's perhaps the most common definition of investigative reporting. But some of the best, and some of the most impactful, reporting can be as simple as getting local health department records on restaurant inspections, or police reports for shopping malls during the holiday season for their "most dangerous mall" annual feature—it's not really that hard.

The bad news for street reporters is that obtaining access to closed "executive sessions" in government meetings, and other traditional rights journalists (and street reporters) have, are always being pushed back by government agencies at every level. Because it is worth the topic of a book in itself—and there are already many of them out there—I am not addressing all that here. But if you are just learning about journalism, you should know that investigative reporting is a wild toboggan ride down the highway of news. It's not for everyone, but the people who love it become, at times, obsessed by it. So, before you even start: Heads up.

Some story ideas are bigger than others. How do you judge that? There are several ways. A good story could involve a lot of money—for example, public money being wasted. Or a good story can be impactful based on the number of people impacted by it, locally or nationally. Sometimes crucial stories are hidden in big piles of statistics collected by government or private corporations, making them harder to find.

What makes something an investigative story rather than just a story? It's true that often an investigative project is considered one that has a lot of different parts that need to be catalogued in some way, more than the normal stories you might do on your beat. But I personally think that what makes one story an investigative story and another story not, is that an investigative project will explain how some important process works in your local community. Or, rather, it will explain why it is not working the way it should be.

Like the story I worked on about a woman whose car was stolen, then turned up for sale two weeks later at a used car lot on a seedy suburban strip miles away. The police bureau notification that the car had been abandoned and retrieved never made it to her hands; the U.S. Postal Service insisted that they put a sticky note on her door about it during a rainstorm. Long into short, she never got her car back. It was a story about the system—not a personality profile or business feature.

Another story I reported was about a woman who was wrongfully accused of shoplifting in a local department store; the department store manager insisted the woman's name had appeared on a "national database of shoplifters." Neither a police officer nor an attorney could force the store into producing her photograph or a "national register of shoplifters;" in fact, as it turns out, there are multiple national registers of shoplifters compiled by different retail industries, and there is no official process for removing anyone from any of these lists; they have no connection to any police bureau. My story explored the private law enforcement process that operated outside the legal system—it was not a "human interest" story about the woman, as nice as she was.

Investigative Reporting Ethics

This humble book does not have the scope to really discuss investigative reporting in depth. But for less trained but aspiring journalists thinking about how to tackle more complicated or impactful issues within their area of interest, here are a few tips. Start here: The only motivation for investigating an organization or individual must be as part of a policy analysis—not for personal reasons.

In investigating and reporting on a person or organization, you cannot make personal attacks, cite personal details, or be motivated by personal experiences; it has to be about a bigger picture somehow, an issue that impacts many people and that someone can perhaps do something about. Personal reasons for collecting information about another person or organization can be grounds for a harassment lawsuit or worse. That is not journalism.

Working in newsrooms with everyday people, I have worried about how much street journalism is fueled by rage. As I left my previous job in the newspaper industry, I felt emotionally traumatized by the difficulty of the stories I had been writing for years—stories about street violence, families losing their homes and businesses, mothers losing their children. It stoked a rage that, in turn, kept me going through long reporting projects.

But the fact is that you might see deep reporting efforts that look to you like good opportunities to get revenge against individuals or corporations or institutions. You need to stop yourself.

This might sound cynical, but part of the reason to be scrupulously fair and accurate in your dealings with people, especially in investigative reporting, is that you are building your personal reputation. If you do a project trying to highlight an underreported health trend or something of that nature in which you feature the work someone is doing to resolve the health problem, you are building at least two relationships: one is with the people (doing something, for a reason, remember?); the other is with your audience, which is consuming all this information you are putting out. Whether good or bad, be aware of that.

When you are scrupulously fair with your sources, you are opening a door that invites whistleblowers—people who see corruption in their workplace or other bureaucracy and want to speak out about it despite certain dangers in doing that. This is one of the most important kinds of sources you can ever have, and you have to set the table in advance for them—again, with your fairness. This is part of building sources in the community.

Freedom of Information Act (FOIA)

The Freedom of Information act, signed into law in 1966, defines the public's right to know about the government agency records and operations. Not just the federal government, but also state governments have rules on freedom of information. In some cases, states have even more exemptions from the law for their government agencies than the federal government itself does. This means that members of the press and also the public of one state may have less rights to know about what the government is doing than other states do.

If you want to get documents from a government agency through the Freedom of Information Act, you should start by finding their website online and looking for a link to "Information Act requests" or something of that nature.

Many government agencies and bureaus have their own systems for requests of this kind, and you can just plug all your information in on their website. You're going to have to look around—there is no standard way these are set out, and plenty of bureaucracies don't really want you to file these requests, so they may be hidden.

Journalists filing Information Act requests are often looking for statistics, dramatic messages, or anything that seems hidden from view. That includes things like documents showing how money was spent by a government agency; or how many people were fatally wounded on the job in a certain national industry; or what the county commissioners are texting to each other during their weekly public meeting. Remember earlier when we talked about being ready with ways to store and organize all the things? That matters now more than ever.

Kinds of Investigative Stories

As a reporter, you can dig deeply into almost anything that interests you. There are, however, a handful of classic investigative projects that are almost always going to lead to an investigation of interest in your area. Not only that, as a journalist, no matter what platform you use, you can establish your own important investigative reporting territory that you continue to cover over time. So, keeping that in mind, you could potentially use each of these kinds of classic investigative projects on one issue over time.

Sometimes, when you're first coming to an investigative project, you're not sure how to tell the story or what investigative tools to use. Or, you see an issue that interests you and seems impactful, but you're not sure how to approach it. That's when it's a good idea to look back on old standards of investigative reporting.

Experiences—Stories Looking at Oppression

Probably the most basic, bread and butter investigative story that you could do right now is setting yourself in some remarkable experience and then writing a feature story about what happened. It's really good to do extra research and take out statistics to bolster whatever it is that you're trying to show, yet the real juice of this approach is that you have to tough something out personally.

The most classic example of experiential investigative reporting is more than one hundred years old, by investigative reporter Nellie Bly. As a reporter for a New York City newspaper, she and her publisher arranged to have her committed to the insane asylum system in that city. As a completely sane person in real life, Bly remained in the mental health facility for women for a week and half, was released, and then wrote an eyewitness account of abuses there.

Her work led to social reforms by the city of New York. Needless to say, the experience—which you can read today for free via Internet download—was harrowing, and at times physically painful, which is part of what makes it such compelling reading even today.

Other "experiential" investigative reporting projects include working a job in a sector considered to be abusive, such as waitressing, house cleaning, or fruit packing factories; ingesting over-the-counter medical products that bring on psychedelic effects but that are not regulated by the medical industry, and then writing about that tripped-out experience; any similar activity with some kind of social justice or corporate accountability frame would probably be of interest.

Helping Someone Who Needs an Advocate

It is my personal experience that the most important and impactful stories come from your readers who call you looking for an advocate in the face of some bureaucratic or legal trap. The documents they bring with them in stuffed manila envelopes and big boxes and rolling suitcases are often the kind of paperwork FOIA doesn't cover. This is why you should have a front door to your operations somehow—a way for people to come in and ask for help.

When you are considering journalistically investigating a government agency in the U.S., first go online to search for the official website of the city, county, state, and federal government agency you're looking for; then click around on homepage links to find the most recent info from each individual agency you are looking at. If you are considering journalistically investigating a private company, you can go online to your local, state government regulatory agency to check their licensing if it is a state or local government-based entity. This would be one of those cases where you would be potentially noting the absence of such a license.

Exploring a Process

This is an interesting evergreen frame for an investigative project. It involves outlining a long process that goes into some important public function, describing all the steps along the way. Reporting that follows the dangerous journeys of migrant workers traveling over the Texas/Mexico border; the Pulitzer Prize-winning series by Richard Read of the *Oregonian* newspaper that followed a shipment of potatoes grown in Oregon all the way around the world to China, where they were processed into frozen french fries; any investigative project that follows what happens to the garbage that we throw out in our garbage cans—and where it ends up. The best ideas in exploring a process show readers and watchers something new about their world that's right under their noses.

Process stories can be a breath of fresh air, and lend themselves to creative storytelling techniques, such as the *New York Times* multimedia series about an avalanche in Washington State. That fascinating project, which included cutting-edge digital film effects, asked the question: How did this avalanche take the lives of two of the most experienced skiers in the world?

Health Department Records

If you are interested in medical issues or public health, there are many directions you could go if you simply delved into your county health department's different divisions. Here is an area where it can be a good idea to make friends with the spokespeople, and then ask their advice on which underreported stories are most crucial within their area of expertise; within the past five years, what used to be a full press corps reporting healthcare has been decimated, leaving many stories untold.

Ask the spokesperson about areas of operations that are important but underreported. That might include county health department restaurant inspection records—how did your favorite restaurant do when the health inspector came by? Other divisions at most county health departments involve tracking disease and illness. What are the most common diseases in your area? What kind of research is being done on those diseases? is a classic project. Since most hospitals deal with the federal patient privacy law known as HIPAA (the Health Insurance Portability and Accountability Act of 1996), you might talk with the hospital spokespeople about what kinds of records you might access regarding trends in your area of interest.

Looking Up Campaign Contributions

The Federal Elections Commission (FEC) is in charge of national campaign finance laws. All presidential candidates have to file reports on the contributions they've received and how much they've spent, and how. If you are covering national races, always check their website first.

In addition, nonprofit, nonpartisan organizations have created easy-to-use and accurate platforms online to dig out campaign contribution information in your local community and nationwide. The best one is called www.opensecrets.org, where you can easily look up which corporations, or individuals, or special interest sectors have made contributions to specific candidates on the federal level that you may be reporting on; you can also discover how much money has changed hands.

On the state level, some local governments have created online platforms where all campaign-finance information is posted; sometimes these data troves can be difficult to read. If you're lucky enough to live in an area where there even is one, it's worth it to take the time to learn how it works. Here is where you can find out who is funding campaigns for mayor, or sheriffs, judges, or supervisors. Is dog catcher an elected office?

Nonprofit Organizations and Private Companies

Wherever you go in the world of journalism, the documents tell the story. Depending on what you are investigating, if it is some kind of institution in the public or private sector, you can start out by thinking about what government agencies regulate that institution. Create a list. Start finding out who runs them and, if you are working on some kind of watchdog project analyzing finances, here is where you can find out how much money they have.

In the case of nonprofit organizations, you can find financial information as well as staffing and contact information for members of boards of directors by looking up what are called Internal Revenue Service 990 filings, on any given state department of justice website. The IRS 990 form is a required tax filing that constitutes the public disclosures of each individual nonprofit organization of the U.S. They are tracked by state governments. They are public records often available online and have information regarding board members, income, contact information, staff, sometimes even cell phone numbers of staff.

Depending on what you are looking at, you could take that information and begin searching the social networks connecting the issue you are investigating. You would be looking for influential people and, literally, the people they're influencing, as they relate to your specific issue that you are researching.

Private Sector Investigative Projects

If you would like to journalistically investigate a private company, your options for obtaining information are severely limited. The U.S. Freedom of Information Act provides a legal framework for residents and members of the media to obtain some forms of information considered to be in the public interest, but it only covers government agencies. More specifics about what documents are or are not covered are mostly decided by Secretaries of State, creating a confusing legal patchwork.

On the other hand, try searching for the name of your corporation within lawsuits filed; legal documents are the best place to find information that would normally be privileged. Get a copy of the legal papers through your local county or state court's computer system, often found in your local courthouse.

EXERCISES

- Just sitting in a chair where you are now, brainstorm three investigations you wish someone would do about issues that affect your life every day. What are those three areas? In each of those areas, what is one question that should be asked? Who should be made to answer?

- Now, to do a little research, look on the Internet for three words relating to the questions you were asking in the previous exercise, plus adding the words "who regulates?" Try to figure out what governmental body regulates activities in the fields that you investigated in the previous exercise. Who are the bosses in this zone?

- Look on their website for documents that pertain to your areas of interest. What are you turning up?

- Compile a list of all of the websites that you just found pertaining to your area of interest. At the top of it, put in any government agencies or private boards that regulate that industry. Next, list all of the nonprofit organizations that serve your industry in some way and figure out which ones are lobbying organizations. Start a spreadsheet listing all of these groups and individuals, making sure that one field of your spreadsheet is their corporate headquarters.

CHECK IT OUT!

Investigative reporter Ida B. Wells started her career in 1887—before it was even a thing. While living in Mississippi, Wells insisted on looking into the causes of death listed for lynching victims she knew, literally checking all the records on file in each case. She discovered that the traditional "mob" excuse for lynchings—that the lynching victims were "guilty of rape" or other sexual offenses—was not born out by documentation.

Rather, legal documents showed most lynchings were motivated by white people making a profit in some way. More recent research has shown lynchings happened more often during bad economic times. Just focusing on this one issue—the documentation for each and every lynching reported in the U.S.—Wells created a platform to dig away at the roots of white supremacy during her lifetime.

TECHNIQUE

Start Organized, Stay Organized

First off, investigative projects are the ones least often done, because they generate a lot of work and then you end up with gigantic piles of information. So, the single biggest piece of advice I give people is: Start organized, stay organized, and wrap up your project with specific targeted goals written out. Ask the basic questions: What's wrong? Why? What have you found out about it? Who is getting confronted? And, what should be done to make it right?

It can sound more complicated than it is; a series of laundry lists attached to a calendar and a digital address book would do it. But the key is—start organized and stay organized.

TECHNIQUE

Break it Down

Once you've amassed a pile of facts, images, and interviews, how do you begin to sort through it and think about what you've got? Here is a laundry list of ways you can break down your information—remember, I suggest that as you break it down, you organize your info into piles or folders of things that are alike or that are about the same thing. So, try tackling your whole pile of content for your project and sorting it by:

- Chronology, or the date things happened. What came first? Then what? Then what?

- Ranking facts by importance. Are there things people need to know about your topic—right now?

- If you're still trying to find patterns in all the information you've gathered, try looking for keywords, and then organizing your material around the most common keywords you turn up. For example, if people rioting in the streets has a bearing on your topic, take a look at the issues and ideas within the world of "rioting in the streets" that seem to turn up the most (one of these will be a song by Pokey La Farge—remember that even if you're researching hard news, art can help explain the story). Decide which of these are most important and group your content around those things.

- Still stuck? Maybe you need an expert source to help you? Try looking for Listservs or Reddit chats or YouTube channels around your issue. Is there a community of people already discussing your interest that you have not heard from yet? Maybe by talking with experts you will gain a new insight that will help you move forward.

CHAPTER 7

PULLING IT ALL TOGETHER AND TELLING THE STORY

"Justice is not a natural part of the lifecycle of the U.S., nor is it a product of evolution; it is always the outcome of struggle." —Keeanga-Yamahtta Taylor, author of *From #BlackLivesMatter to Black Liberation*, published by Haymarket Books

Y ou've zeroed in on the story or issue you think is most important to tell. You've gathered information, statistics, pictures, and video of a whole array of people impacted by your issue. Now, what do you do with all this stuff? The purpose of this chapter is to show you a few ways to organize your story—and your information—within a journalistic project.

YOU WILL LEARN:

- Your first step in processing information is culling out the absolutely most important things from your pile of facts and materials.
- Organize items using the Kitty Litter Theory of news organization; start piling up all of your materials clumped up by subject matter, putting like items together.
- Don't be the reporter who vomits information into the zone to get revenge.
- Use writing formats to free your mind for focusing on the content; turn to the format again if you feel your story isn't working.

Years ago, I was hired as a news editor at a community newspaper where a young reporter had already been working several years. This young reporter had a journalism degree from a respected college, but he was convinced that he didn't know how to write. He had already worked with three previous news editors at this newspaper, and they all told him that.

As I looked at his work, it seemed clear that he was a master of information gathering, interviews, photographs, video—the whole nine. It was just organizing his thoughts on paper that was frustrating to him. Armed by these observations, our boss then set him up with a webinar about news writing structures, which are the ways you organize information on the page.

In the webinar, the writing coaches described a typical news story as shaped like a martini glass, with:

- a wide open top bringing in the story topic,
- narrowing down to an important sharp point on what's important about it,
- and ending with the strong base that explores the future of that topic.

After this reporter sat through that webinar, he went on to win almost every journalism award in our newspaper's professional organization. He never looked back at the years when people told him he could not write, because all it took was one moment for him to understand story structures that can save you time and help you focus.

Yes, You Can Write

A lot of people think that you have to be a natural-born writer to succeed as a journalist, but if you master a handful of news writing techniques, you could be a fine news reporter. Just as important as the writing itself is the ability to organize your thoughts and thus how you tell your story. Remember from the previous chapter, all information only comes in six flavors—it's how you stack them up that sets you apart.

When I say "processing information," what I'm talking about is taking all of the facts and materials that you gathered in the last chapter and pulling them all together in one package that makes sense. You're doing this in such a way that the people you're communicating with understand the story you're trying to tell.

In many ways, this is where the art of reporting comes in. Sifting through the information and materials you gathered in this journey towards the story, you must have come upon a handful of truths—facts or ideas that seem to underpin everything you understand about this topic. What is it that you most want to hold up for the world to see about this thing you have been researching?

Before you start, when it comes time to take hold of research you've been doing and pull together all the things you've been collecting to write out your story, don't forget snacks. If you take the time to ensure you can sit at a workstation for hours at a time with comfort food by your side, I guarantee you will get more done. If there is a reason why you perhaps are trying to change your diet to include healthier choices, this is also a crucial time to have those healthy choices right there.

Picture it: You are staring at a throbbing computer screen, the blue light shining upon your face. Some celery stalks with peanut butter can keep you grounded and focused on what you're trying to do. Or gigantic-sized candy bars, ice cream, ham sandwiches with Swiss cheese and arugula. For myself, when I think ahead with treats, even something as simple as a pot of tea with lots of sugar in it, I get more done in the end.

What's Most Important?

Your first step in processing information is culling out the absolutely most important things from your pile of facts and materials. You might be completely overwhelmed by all the stuff you have gathered. But you only have one job right now: Sort through it and rank it in order of importance. You have to find a way to do that so it makes sense to you.

Have you been working on a project for the past six months and now have about five hundred pages of text and twenty hours of audio and fifty hours of video to review? How should you sort through it? What are the best ways to organize and store multimedia files for a single project?

Before you get to that point, it's best if you could figure out some consistent way of labeling all of the audio or video you are collecting for your media project. It almost does not matter what information you include in the labels on each file or the labels on the folders the files are in. It only matters that there's a way to sort through the separate pieces.

Organizing What You've Got

Sorting through the many parts of your media project and organizing them for easiest use is a lot like putting away your laundry. Just as a general principle, you should fiddle with each object as little as possible—visualize juggling each piece into its proper place with the least amount of fuss.

One tool for organizing information for a news story would be through a timeline. Depending on what the story is, or what information you're tracking, trying to arrange the pieces chronologically is often a good idea to start with.

Another quick and easy organizational scheme is ranking by importance. First, decide what are the handful of most important things that you need to make your readers or listeners or watchers understand about the topic you've chosen to cover, and take a moment to think about your overall goal with the project. Is it a consumer protection issue you're raising awareness about? Are you recounting the history of a civil rights effort by an oppressed group within your community? Or perhaps are you on the scene of the breaking news incident such as a street demonstration or a building on fire? First decide what kind of story you want to tell.

Next, try the Kitty Litter Theory of news organization: start piling up all of your materials clumped up by subject matter, putting like items together. For example, one pile might be "history," another pile might be about a specific famous person, one might be "future trends." A typical pile might include a couple of audio interviews on SoundCloud, some photos uploaded to Flickr, a spreadsheet and a text document—they are all radically different platforms, right? But once you assemble all of these pieces, it might only take a few hours to create a beautiful multimedia page telling a compelling story with images and sound.

Get Started with a Grounding in News

Start your path to news writing by reading. Read every newspaper you can get your hands on and familiarize yourself with all the issues you can. As you go, think about the different styles of writing that you are reading. Pull out the ones that resonate with you and ask yourself what it is that you like about them. Is it something about the writing itself? Or is it possibly something to do with the subject matter? Do certain subject matters lend themselves to certain styles of coverage?

Sometimes, after you have sifted through all of your materials and assigned chunks of information to separate sections, you might need to find one common thread you can use to weave together all of the different sections and make them one, unified whole.

This can be a great place to introduce field audio or video that you or your colleagues have recorded to perhaps tell some important story that is part of this coverage. When you are able to present your boring, prerecorded interviews alongside good quality sound from the side of the freeway or the center of a bird sanctuary, the overall effect literally becomes more than the sum of its parts.

When it comes to street reporting, or any kind of reporting, using all of your senses is crucial. In the last two chapters, we talked about information gathering and how to get information from interviewing people. All of that is important, but it's not the whole story. For people who want to dig deeper and tell their story in a different way, take a moment to check your own personal physical senses as you are reporting. Where are you standing? What does it smell like? How does it feel? What sounds are there? What do you see? Always make note of these items because there can be times when they give you new ideas and directions in your project.

Other Tools

- Now that you know the point of your story and what it is about, start plotting out a timeline. As you look at this story, what happened when? You will be surprised at aspects of your story that leap out at you when you look at them from a different point of view, such as the chronological description of events.

So, if you can sketch out for yourself the what-happened-when of what you're investigating as you go, you might have already written your story by the time you're done sifting through the facts.

- Take a minute and ask yourself if there is any sort of database of information that could be used to tell this story. In other words, is there a pile of numbers somewhere that could illuminate the points you're trying to look at? For example, if you are wondering how effectively your city government collects or administers parking tickets and parking ticket fines, you might ask what kind of statistics are kept by the city about that. With a Freedom of Information Act request, you would soon be in possession of those statistics.

- For such a thing as law enforcement numbers, you might consider an interesting way to really show them using bar graphs or line graphs. There are low cost, online platforms like Canva, Vizualize, and even Google Charts where you can upload an Excel spreadsheet and have it automatically rolled into a graphic.

- Also along those lines, one last platform I use a lot in reporting is digital maps, including Google Maps. For this you need complete physical addresses—snail mail addresses, not URLs. Plugging these into an Excel spreadsheet makes it possible to create a variety of graphics including satellite maps, walking tours, business directories, murder trends, community changes through gentrification, and anything else that you can think of that it would be possible to show through a map.

People's Right to Privacy

As you pursue your story, there may be times when you have interviews with or other information about people and you're not sure whether you should use them or not. This can become a hot button question because broadcast media reporting or other online postings can act like weapons, destroying the lives of innocent people. Don't be the reporter who vomits information into the digisphere with a sense of revenge. That's not journalism. On a personal note, I would also strongly encourage would-be journalists not to harass public figures or elected officials by screaming at them or shoving cameras into their faces. That is also not journalism.

An under-discussed area of personal privacy in community journalism is reporting on the stories of vulnerable people. There are limits on law enforcement agencies' ability to reveal the names of juveniles charged with alleged crimes (unless they are charged in adult court). There are also self-imposed news media policies of not revealing the names of victims of sexual assault.

To that list of don'ts, I tend to add publishing the names of people with mental illness arrested and/or charged with crimes in our local community, if we can; it's not always possible to determine the mental state by reading the police reports. That's because I personally would prefer not to compound the overwhelming stigmatization people living with mental illness struggle under every day.

What to Include in a Story and What Not

This is a weird question to ask, because of course wouldn't you want to include all the information you could? But the fact is it's not unusual to gather a large body of information together and then feel unsure about some aspects of it that may seem personal or invasive in regard to individuals you might be reporting about.

It's worth it to take a few moments to evaluate what you have in your reporting package and make sure you're not damaging any individuals in your story. By and large, staying away from people's personal lives is important because in the 21st century, you can cause real harm to real people with your goddamned blog. And that is the kind of damage that is impossible to completely reverse.

If you are doing a feature story about a family with kids, make sure you get their permission before you put their children's images in your media project. Sometimes families have real reasons to fear that. The same can be true of families with extremely elderly relatives, especially if those relatives are in a care facility. Ask before you include their names in a report.

It goes without saying that if you are intentionally trying to personally damage any individual with your reporting, that's not journalism.

Story Structures

The most important thing that separates the good from the great is the art of telling the story—setting the scene with descriptive words or pictures or sounds and bringing the reader, viewer, or listener right to the place where the news is happening.

Having said that, most news reporting boils down to two kinds of stories: breaking news or news features.

Breaking News

Breaking news is like going to the grocery store, in a way. You're in a rush; you only have time for the basics. What's ready to go right now? Here is how to structure your breaking news story:

- In the first paragraph, you list who, what, when, where, how and why.
- In the second paragraph, you state in one sentence why it's important—the larger point of this situation, also known as the "nut graph" of your story.
- The third paragraph should be a quote from someone on the scene describing something about it so important or remarkable that you yourself couldn't sum it up better—especially describing the feelings of people, or the physical sensation of being there, or the bottom line of how it has hit people—from a unique, witness-style point of view.
- And then in each paragraph after that, you list the seven or eight most important things that readers, listeners, or viewers need to know about it. Lists, lists, lists. Like grocery lists, but in complete sentences, right?

It's called breaking news because it's about an emergency situation where there's a sense of urgency that the facts get out.

Features: More Detail

In the feature format, there's more room to set the scene for a story and to delve into the background of your situation. This is where you can bring in more of the voices of people affected by it—maybe even more information about the scene where it happened.

Here's a recipe for that:

- If you are getting ready to put together a piece of media in a feature format, start with one sentence written down which is the point of the story. This is called the nut graph.

- Now come up with between one and three paragraphs to serve as the introduction to the story; this is called the lead. Hopefully it's setting the scene in a way that brings the reader to the nut graph—the single sentence that explains the whole point of the story.
- Then, string together the story as it unfolded, then the seven or eight most important things people should know about the topic.
- Last of all, build a conclusion which either brings the reader/listener/viewer back to the original scene to drive the point home, or perhaps offers information allowing some sort of human interaction, such as an invitation to a community or otherwise public event.

Now/Then/Now Structure

The best feature writing teacher I ever had said the most basic feature format is *now*, *then*, *now*. We're still talking about how to organize your story. This idea calls for a historical piece of the story after the nut graph, specifically. That piece can be as long as it wants to be, or as short as it wants to be. This means the storyteller starts the story with whatever is happening now, followed by some historical perspective of where this thing has been in the past, then bringing the story back to some aspect of the present by the time it ends. Or, conversely, you could arrange your story as then, now, then, which would allow the storyteller to start the story sometime in the past, bring it up to date with something happening now, but then end back with the original scene in the past. Go berserk with that. But I often find that a few constraints are much easier than complete freedom, for writing if nothing else.

Break the Rules

The late journalist Charles Bowden's book *Murder City: Ciudad Juarez and the Global Economy's New Killing Fields* masterfully weaves together his many years of reporting on the drug trade in Latin America. A hard-bitten journalist who had seen countless murders on his beat, Bowden used poetry, harsh facts, and a flowing style to tell the stories of a few inmates of a mental facility in Mexico near where he was staying. Using deeper, even literary tools of storytelling rather than a top-down description of events gives a deeper understanding of the situation. Bowden broke all the rules in order to tell the story his own way.

If you are ready to think about your reporting project from a different point of view, start by trying to write down elements of the story that are in your mind, the way you see them or perhaps hear them. Go ahead and use the format of a laundry list or a timeline—no need for complete sentences. Or try drawing pictures, like a comic strip; stick figures are fine.

One more aspect to throw into your mix: If you are working in an audio or visual medium, recording from some remote or otherwise especially unexpected location can give your audience a fun opportunity to get out of the space they are in right then. Almost any kind of mobile device can live stream the situation you're in, which allows you to bring your audience with you. There are so many different ways to do that; one can only assume in the future we'll be heating our breakfasts and washing the dog with the same device that live streams today's riot against the government.

Challenge Yourself

If you want to effectively harness the power of new media, it's worth it to make a list of the social media platforms that carry your medium—photos? Cartoons? Videos? Podcasts? Take the time to figure out where you want your personal output to live online and stay on top of advancements in that zone.

Once you have your list of which sites do exactly what, examine the materials you have, including your equipment. Do you have any videos, photographs, or other digital recordings that would fit the format for any of these platforms right now? Next question: Do you have a camera or smartphone or tablet that is capable of taking photographs or video so that you could begin flushing out a social media platform?

Find one place where you can save or store as much of the material you have gathered as possible. Chances are that virtually everything you would need to create a reported story could be gathered together on a computer hard drive. Now, find out how big each of these media items tends to be. You might need to purchase an extra hard drive or an online platform like a personal blog or website. This is a point when you stop and make a list of what different kinds of multimedia files you are using and how you will weave them together. There will be more on this in Chapter 10, "Platforms: Building Your Place in the Journalism World."

EXERCISES

- Take all of your notes and content (including interviews from the exercises you did in the last chapter) and highlight them according to now, then, and now. By that I mean: "now," where you describe what is going on right this minute with your issue; "then," where you outline the history for your topic; and "near future," in which you describe the immediate future or outcome of the situation you are reporting on. Divide all of your notes into documents with file names that contain those three categories: now, then, and near_future. Store your pieces in a safe folder on a secure computer and consider backing it up on a thumb drive.

- Create a spreadsheet listing everyone you interviewed for this important story that includes social media links and best contact information. Consider creating a thoughtful organizational plan for your general contacts; you would be surprised at how often they come back around.

CHECK IT OUT!

The idea of "crowdsourcing" is to take a problem or puzzle and ask for public help in solving it. In journalism, the idea of crowdsourcing information usually involves a media outlet making a public call for information of a specific kind for a story. This is what *Washington Post* reporter David Farenthold did in a Twitter call to veterans' organizations to ask if any of them had received any contribution from Donald J. Trump; the answer was no. Another example is the Panama Papers, an open trove of global finance documents gathered by the International Consortium of Investigative Journalists and then arranged online in a searchable format, so anyone can log on and search lists of corporations using fake fronts to cheat on their taxes. Other projects around the world have included quality control on eldercare facilities, textbook quality, and tracking fatalities and injuries in war zones.

CHAPTER 8

FACT-CHECKING

"The most important ethical issues and the most difficult ones are the human ones, because a reporter has enormous power to hurt people."
—Carl Bernstein

F act checking is what lets the people who consume your story know that it wasn't made with rotten eggs and rancid milk. It's like stopping the grocery cart one last time before you head to the checkout line to make sure the $20 worth of butter you grabbed really matches the half-off coupon. With every piece of information you weave into your story, there will be a need—and a way—to double-check that item and make sure it is accurate, and this is a step you are *not allowed* to skip.

The purpose of this chapter is to teach methods of fact-checking and personal editing that can be useful in your writing every day. Also, we'll look closer at the limits of what we think of as "facts."

YOU WILL LEARN:

- Fact-checking is not a question of doing it or not doing it—it's a question of laying the groundwork for accuracy from the time you start out with your first idea and throughout your project.
- Sometimes the facts can be debated—find out how and when.
- Come up with your own self-editing checklist and use it every time.
- Fact-checking for cultural bias is difficult to do if your media project is being put together by a homogenous crew—it won't be "true" unless you seek out more perspectives.

When it comes to fact-checking, there are many things we can agree on that are the basic facts of the story. That would include names, dates, government agencies, and specific laws. Most of the time, when you are working on a story or project, it is easy enough to come up with a checklist of items you want to make sure you do not mess up. In fact, if you are working with a team of people, a laundry list of items to double-check would be an excellent communications tool you can share with your entire team. On the other hand, there are stories in which the facts, as people can agree on them, shift. For the purposes of fact-checking, by and large, government documents can serve as an original source of baseline information. But are they always actually accurate?

Basic accuracy is something not necessarily taught in journalism school. I don't recall any class in fact-checking, more a vague threat: You better do it. Now, many years later, I see the issue of fact-checking as multifaceted. It's not a question of do it or not do it, it's a question of laying the groundwork for accuracy from the time you start out with your first idea and throughout your project.

It's more than spelling people's names right; it's also checking in deeply with the culture you're writing about to make sure you understand what the information you have actually means. Sometimes mistakes happen, and a worthy goal as a journalist is to make sure that any obvious mistakes in your project have not compounded into some gigantic error in judgment that plays out in your final product. It has your name on it, right?

There is no established industry standard for fact-checking; media outlets each tend to have their own style. A few years ago, a small team of academics published a rare research paper showing that variety in approach was the rule. Journalist and fact-checking expert Craig Silverman outlined the research paper and explained it this way:

"The researchers found that verification is widely seen as essential and core to a journalist's work. But at the same time, the methods for achieving accuracy vary from one journalist to the next. There is no single standard for verification, and not every fact is treated the same. A small, easily checkable fact needs to be checked; a larger but greater assertion, not so much—unless it is defamatory, " they write. "Thus, verification for a journalist is a rather different animal from verification in scientific method, which would hold every piece of data subject to a consistent standard of observation and replication."

Create Your Own System

That's why sitting down and thinking about your values and work as a journalist will put you in the driver's seat to drawing up your own policies and procedures for fact-checking that fit the kind of work that you personally do. If you are a writer specializing in food carts, bookstores, or community centers, you could start out by making a telephone and email spreadsheet with the names of people you need in your community, other contact information that you need, and any other important information.

If, on the other hand, you are primarily using Twitter as the main platform for getting out your personal messages, you might build a series of Twitter lists. Consider building up databases or lists that have themes to organize the contact information of your sources. That way, if you're running through your self-editing checklist and you need to contact someone, all the information is in one place.

It's a Process

Often when people think about fact-checking for a piece of media, they think about picking it up after it's all done and looking up each piece of information that's in it. But actually, fact-checking starts at the very beginning of your reporting, when you choose what information to include as the basis for your project. By and large, when it comes to a deep and intense investigative news project, as you already know, documents tell the story.

That means as much as you want to believe all the nice people who contact you with touching stories of wrongdoing by big institutions, their word is not enough. In the case of members of the public who bring important stories to you, ask them to provide the documentation of what they're saying. For me, a lot of important stories start this way.

Fact-check Like You Mean It

Don't try to write an important story from a distance. Go out and talk to people involved in the issue to get a bottom line; read all you can on the facts you are dealing with.

Don't just mash together what you have read elsewhere online or on TV; build relationships with all of the people you speak with. They are called "sources." If you are just starting out in creating your own reporting platform, consider researching spokespeople of local government agencies that pertain to that issue.

Try to reach out and make a connection with the spokespeople, because they will become key pipelines of the information you really need. Never be rude to a front desk receptionist of any agency or business that you need to get information from; realize from the get-go the front desk receptionist is often the nerve center of their entire office. If you need a genuine fact-check of your information—not necessarily confirmation on the record—a front desk receptionist can be a valuable source.

Make Lists

Be sure to keep a complete log of all the websites you visit, all the searches you make, Google alert results, and anything else that you think is useful, connected to your specific topic. That way, when you are coming back through all of your words and all of your chapters, you'll have an easier time finding this specific article or documentary you have cited in your project.

The beauty of building these items into Excel or Google spreadsheets is that under certain circumstances, you can take the same spreadsheet you have been using as a contact sheet, upload it to a website, and then press a button to turn it into a graphic image. That includes maps, bar graphs, and more.

Please note that keeping your information in spreadsheets is a strategic gamble and that the corporation that owns one of them will create ways of preserving your stuff for years to come. But keeping your digital information in one place can sometimes be a way of holding on to it as times change.

Back to the Facts

This is a good time to talk about defining what is a fact. It might sound obvious, but it actually is not. There are things that we know to be true—but then there are the things we can check up on using official records. Those two things might not be the same.

Say, for example, a young man was arrested by police in his apartment. He has his version of events, but the police have their own, which is written into the police report. Which version of events is a fact? That depends on whether charges are brought against the man as a result of the police report and whether there is a conviction in the case.

As a journalist, avoid repeating anything people have said to you without checking it out, especially regarding a lawsuit or legal charges. If you are working on a story about a lawsuit, it's extra important to make sure every single thing you report is backed up by paperwork, some sort of testimony or document filed in the case—something you can hold in your hand.

Think about it: If you're in the middle of a bunch of people who have lawyered up, they're already dealing out lawsuits like jelly beans, and they might as well give one to you too. Actions that you might take as a street journalist in covering a legal case could potentially damage that case, and for that reason, you should pay particularly close attention to what you're doing.

Where Racism, Sexism, Bigotry Get In

Another thing to watch out for, often detailed in Craig Silverman's now discontinued but still readable blog Regret the Error has to do with misunderstandings between reporters and the people that we interview. That could include anything from a simple lack of clarity during an interview to unintended false reporting through exaggerated memories of "good people"—failing to apply critical analysis in examining respected figures. For example, a former governor of Oregon raped a teenaged girl for years, but the story wasn't reported until the woman was in her forties; the governor was such a powerful leader for economic growth and urban development that the daily newspaper at the time simply declined to pursue the story until they were shamed into it by an alternative weekly.

In other words, aside from self-editing checklists, there are some errors that seem more like mistakes in judgment than of facts. This area also touches on the problems of racism and cultural competency—the ability to do your job in a way that serves people across cultures and ultimately benefits everyone in society. In other words, if you are a white reporter trying to cover an issue or story from a community of color, you might not actually understand what the story is really about because you may not know anything about that culture—including the ways you are interconnected with it.

One thing I always do is stop and make myself look at the whole story from another point of view. Remember when we talked about "touchstones?" Fact-checking for cultural bias is difficult to do if your media project is being put together by an all-white crew—it won't be "true" unless you seek out more perspectives. This is the time to check in with them.

Check Your Checklist for Assholery

Start with a well-rounded personal editing checklist. There are many boilerplate ones online; take one of those and then add a handful of the errors that you yourself tend to make. As you compile this list for yourself, you can also ask questions of interpretation. You might think, my quotes seem to make so-and-so look bad; is he or she really a bad person?

In fact, included on that checklist should be to stop before you publish and think about how it will impact all the people named in it. Is there a vulnerable person in your story? Take extra time to examine what impacts your reporting will have on vulnerable people. Mitigate the harm or don't report at all. This is the single most important thing you will do.

"Hit and Run" Journalism

Plenty of times, articles that seem sensationalistic in the digital media end up damaging everyday people's lives because some of the basic facts were wrong. This is one reason why I try to notify every person named in an article that they are in it and in what context. Don't be one of those hit and run journalists who does damage then disappears. How are the issues affecting the people named in your story? What other points of view about the issues here could there be?

Sometimes thinking this way leads me to other sources I had not considered before. It's always worth it to shift your perspective before you finish, even if you change your mind back eventually. Above all, try to find some interesting inspiration from seeking a new perspective.

Careful on Unions

Along those lines, I wanted to cite specifically the area of organized labor. Organized labor is one of the most difficult areas I've ever reported on. The worst error I ever made as a reporter was in my very first newspaper job. I was working on a story about organized labor. I had a lunch meeting with three local teachers' union members back in the 1980s. They were telling me everything that was wrong with where they worked, and everything they were going to do about it now that they were in charge of their union shop. We ate sandwiches, I took notes, and they all talked the whole time.

Although I did fact-check, I fact-checked the wrong questions with the wrong people. I should have been more organized, double-checked everything that was said, and looked up the law regulating what the union women were allowed to say publicly. When the story came out, I was officially chastised before the school board of the city for violating confidentiality agreements between the district and the union.

The women that I had interviewed backpedaled as fast as they could from our meeting and our interview; if possible, they were in even more trouble than I was. Which brings us to another common mistake made by new reporters: the idea of "just reporting what people say." Under certain situations, that approach could land you in court with a defamation suit (please see section on libel and slander, below).

Tools for Fact-checking

In my personal experience, fact-checking is the first step in not being screamed at by angry people. In journalism, mistakes will definitely be made. No one is perfect. But there are concrete ways to organize your quality control efforts the same way you organize your notes, email correspondence, and daily to-do lists.

This might seem like a strange idea, but when you go back to the concept that our media outlets are nothing but information factories, you can see that it's possible to create quality control processes for information just like for cookies on an assembly line.

The key is to draw up a self-editing checklist, which includes a specific roster of the kinds of facts you, personally, most often mess up or stress out about in your reporting work. Are you a bad speller? Do you use a lot of math? Are you worried that all of the financial statistics in your series on corporate corruption cases might be accurate? Write it all down and then check each item off as you double-check your story. You can reuse the same self-editing checklist every time.

Tape It If You Can

One last thing. When I started getting serious about covering the city council, I started recording almost every single interview I did with people. I would write my stories by transcribing the audio, and I would keep the MP3 file of the audio in a folder in my computer.

Making the choice to record all of your big interviews is in many ways a pain in the ass. That's because once you make that interview recording, the implication is you'll have to listen to the whole thing again—that makes it time-consuming in some cases.

The other thing to think about when planning to record all your interviews is where are you storing your important digital files? You need some place with a lot of room, and you might as well think about it in advance. If you are one of the old-school reporters who chooses only to use written notes, you will be able to store all of those little notebooks in one cardboard box that you could leave in your carport. The problem with them is they're harder to move and subject to damage from cats and bugs.

Building Community

I am repeating a few points here. If you're serious about building community around your work, then consider drawing up a plan to make a connection with the maximum number of people in your zone. And if you want to stay in a good relationship with them, then let them know if you put them on the air or in your pages.

You should definitely consider contacting everyone named in your story with a description of their role in the story and any quote of theirs for them to verify. Remember to be fair and treat people the way you would like to be treated if it was you, dragged through the mud publicly.

Although, having said that, the fact is even seeing yourself in the newspaper or on the web is a shock to people. Being in the limelight is no casual matter, and if you are a grassroots journalist trying to cover a local community and you expect that community to interact with you, it's your responsibility to help the people that you're covering become comfortable with your work.

Should you send out copies of your story to be read in advance by the people that you wrote about? Most people do not, but I personally have done this to avoid blindsiding innocent people who could be damaged by it.

What Are Libel and Slander?

Generally speaking, libel is a written statement about an individual or organization or community casting them in a negative light in such a way as to damage them economically or in some other measurable way. Slander is the same situation except where the statement is spoken rather than written.

Suing a journalist or media outlet in the U.S. for defamation involves different requirements of the law for private residents versus "public figures."

Private residents suing for defamation need to prove three things:

- that wrong information was transmitted publicly,
- that it was harmful to the victim, and

- that it's the fault of the journalist or the media outlet or whomever is being sued.

For a public figure to sue for defamation, they must prove these three standards and also that the statements were made with "actual malice"—that someone wanted revenge. Which, in the case of some blogs, that's not so hard to do. In other words, it's not always what you said/wrote/sang, but also all the other mean things you said leading up to that one objectionable thing.

EXERCISES

- For one week, keep track of all the corrections in the *New York Times*. Are there any patterns?
- Start binge-reading journalism columns by Craig Silverman, of Regret the Error. Silverman is a journalist and an expert on fact-checking in journalism. He has studied and reported about how to debunk Internet hoaxes in his 2014 book, *The Verification Handbook*. Look up Silverman's examples of how to make a self-editing checklist and try making your own, paying special attention to journalistic errors you feel you are prone to making.
- If you are working on a reporting project, get into the habit of storing links to every page you visit on a single online document connected to your project. Sometimes when you get to the end of your work and you're trying to shuffle quickly through the large pile of items, you find yourself at the mercy of your own filing system. So make it easy to remember and save yourself a lot of time down the road.

CHECK IT OUT!

One of the great examples of street journalism was the school food reform crusade of a nine-year-old schoolgirl in Scotland. Martha Payne, on a blog she created in 2012 with a little bit of help from her father, simply posted a photo of her daily school lunch.

Within weeks, the meals she shared—one in particular was pizza, mashed potatoes-in-a-crust, and canned corn—triggered outrage for their lack of nutrition and often-disgusting presentation. The blog, called NeverSeconds, attracted more than one million followers, was censored and nearly shut down by her local government, then championed by the Scottish education minister. Payne declined donations, instead passing them on to a charity in Africa that provides school lunches to children.

TECHNIQUE

Make Friends with Facts

Use your fact-checking process to make friends in the community of people you are reporting on. What does that look like?

It means using a pleasant tone of voice when you call them on the phone, laying out for them in advance the most controversial parts of the story and asking the person depicted in them to comment and give their side.

That doesn't mean whitewashing their character—just be aboveboard in your dealings and don't cut corners here. You never know who is a gatekeeper today that might become the whistleblower of tomorrow, especially with a spokesperson of an organization that you may suspect is guilty of some bad doings. Also, once the "bad people" are gone, you will still be on the job, trying to get information out of that spokesperson.

The way I look at it, we're all essentially desperate, lonely people sitting at computers. No reason not to reach out as human beings.

STORY IDEA

Fact-checker

Speaking of fact-checking, one kind of story that never goes out of date is checking the corrections sections of major media to look for really big whoppers, which generally become what are called "follow-up" stories. Once a story has run in a major media outlet, whether it has mistakes or not, most people never see any follow up.

But you can leap over the barrier by pulling together completely new coverage of an important issue if you see patterns—or, again, real big errors—in media corrections sections. Craig Silverman, in his fact-checking blog Regret the Error, reported on a *New York Times* reporter in South America who triggered so many corrections that it became clear he was falsifying entire stories. Make it a habit to check the corrections section and see what you get from it over time.

CHAPTER 9

CREATING YOUR VOICE AS A JOURNALIST

The goal of this chapter is to help you find your own individual style as a journalist, whether as a writer or digital broadcaster. This includes choosing your area of interest, working on the sound of your voice, and the style of your presentation.

By now, you have taken ideas and used them to mine information that's important to the public. You've taken the information and whipped it up into narratives that tell a story your audience can understand and relate to. It's time for you to take the next step and really claim your own niche in the media world by deciding who you are and what you stand for.

Corporate marketing people might call it your "brand," but everyday people might describe it as your personal style—which can include a lot of areas, such as your communication style, your vocabulary, your politics, your music or clothing. Any or all of these areas of personal identity can and will become part of your identity as a journalist.

YOU WILL LEARN:

- The sound of your voice, and how you use it, can sometimes have more of an impact on your listenership than the quality of your content.
- The first way to define your voice is to pay careful attention to the tone of the information you curate onto your media platform.
- Unless your newsroom or book collaborators includes people from different backgrounds, you are missing out in terms of understanding basic issues you're reporting on.
- And how far you will go in advocating for other people?

No matter what your area of interest is, <u>one of the most important</u> <u>things you should pay attention to is your voice</u>. By your voice I don't necessarily mean your sound, but rather your whole style of communicating with the public through your media outlet. People all over the world love to engage with thoughtful minds on topics of common interest. The question is how will you present yourself to the world? Broadcast journalism definitely requires a little bit of show business; the sound of your voice, and how you use it, can have more of an impact on your listenership than the quality of your content. Finding your own personal writing or broadcasting voice will involve weaving together your depth of knowledge with, literally, a sound that is pleasing or at least compelling to the ear.

Another surprising part of finding your journalistic voice has to do with who you talk to, and who you are working with. Unless your newsroom or book collaborators include people from different backgrounds, you are missing out in terms of understanding basic issues you're reporting on. From transportation to healthcare to culture, you will be missing out in terms of reaching a wider array of readers or watchers or listeners.

My sweetheart is a vaudeville performer, and he comes from a long tradition of people who juggle and dance and clown around to make audiences laugh. In that vaudeville community, the performers have a saying: Everything that happens on stage is part of the show. The same is true in radio and television and other forms of broadcast media. Did guns go off? Did the police pepper spray everything? Did someone walk through and shout the F-word? Part of what makes journalism so remarkable is that you, the creator, get to visualize the entire project from beginning to end––what it looks like, what it sounds like, the language of it.

You are helping create parts of the public record of what happened in the history of where you are right now. I think this is one of the most important things for newcomers to understand, as you are dreaming of your own media platform sharing the fruits of your research and documentation on the subject most important to you.

Years from now, when young people and newcomers are trying to figure out what happened in their past, they're going to find your website loaded with all of your interviews and photographs and videos and assume what's there is exactly what happened.

Share the Mic

I would like to personally strongly advocate for finding a way to take the microphone out of your hand and get it into the hands of people who least often get access to media—people from underserved and marginalized communities. Taking that one step towards equity will grow the sound and the reach of whatever you're doing.

Your Substance and Style

Perhaps the first way to define your voice is to pay careful attention to the tone of the information you curate onto your media platform. I don't just mean links to other articles or books that reflect your interest, but also the kinds of questions that you ask as you gather information out in the world. The images that you include are also part of your voice.

As you approach your subject of interest, over time you'll create a track record in how you "break things down." That means how you evaluate information in your zone, how you judge its importance for your audience, and potentially also what kind of community you build around your information platform.

This really is a significant part of your voice as a journalist—the sources you cultivate and how you communicate them to your readers, listeners and/or viewers.

Here is another repeated point: For myself, I have looked around my zone and created a community advisory board whose judgment helps me do my job. This is absolutely necessary, in my personal opinion. It is an extra step of input to weave in voices from communities that are affected by the stories I work on.

Thinking in Advance of Who You Are

If you are just starting a new podcast, or some other kind of broadcast program, chances are you have outlined your project in detail. Subject matter, format, staffing needed, maybe even theme music. If you are just starting out as a broadcast news reporter, or features reporter, you may have already filed a few stories with a serious voice, or perhaps with a jocular voice. You are beginning to also get the sense of your own reporting voice.

Wherever you are on the spectrum, you should take a moment to stop and write down a list of words to describe what you want to be personally projecting as a broadcast journalist. Fun, bright, uplifting? Great! Serious, authoritative, accurate? Excellent! Before you even start with the work you would love to do with your life, think about the image you want to project with your social media, your blog posts, everything you do in public. All of these things will be wrapped together in a package for everyone who searches your name online.

Another very specific thing you should consider in advance is how far you will go in advocating for other people. One of the things that happens when you create a media platform and that platform becomes more and more prominent is that people start coming to you asking for jobs, and media coverage, and financial contributions. If you are a do-gooder, you might think before you start about what kind of contributions you might make to emerging nonprofit organizations within your community.

Make It Work for You

If you are able to take the time to brainstorm your own ideas for what you want to create using your media platform and your message, you will also be in a position to dream up fun, catchy ideas that could set you apart from your competition. To begin with, read over boring news stories until your voice has a calm, deep, intelligent tone; listen to recordings of it back until you're able to hear it and it sounds good.

Now, think about your name and how it sounds when you say it out loud. Say it until you hear it in a way that you like, and then stick that inside your mind to do it again later.

At this point, just to recap, you have a strong reading voice that sounds good in a broadcast because you have worked on it, and you have a nice-sounding style for delivering your name on the air.

Depending on what kind of program you are producing, there's another thing you could do for fun: come up with your own personal tagline, a handful of words that you deliver at some point in your broadcast, perhaps at the very end. A dear friend of mine who once hosted and produced a three-hour-long Saturday radio show with interviews and also blocks of music, had a handful of charming taglines he would use every week––some inherited from the renowned original host of that show, who had since passed away.

There are many broadcast hosts with famous turns of speech linked just to them. As a writer or a reporter or broadcast producer, you actually have more power than other people around you over information. If you look ahead, you might come up with some fun, productive idea that would actually build up the people around you and inspire them.

If you are producing some sort of broadcast, at the very least, before you record your first episode, write out a uniform introduction for your show. Write a catchy introduction followed by your name and all the other credits that you need to say at the beginning of the show. Start off each episode in a focused manner so that people won't lose interest in the first ten seconds.

Using Voices to Paint a Picture

As you look around you for ideas on how to pursue a specific project that you may be considering––perhaps you have found an important story that has been overlooked in the popular attention, something compelling and worth broadcasting––consider organizing your program around the voices you have recorded for this story.

Of course, you will have recorded other kinds of sound as well; all of those other sounds are important in setting the scene of your story and bringing your listeners and watchers with you to that scene.

What I mean is that as you are visualizing the larger sweep of your project––whether it is a sports feature, or investigative series, or a long slideshow about pets at the Humane Society––consider starting your brainstorms on your reporting by sketching out which interviews you have with people involved in your research.

Personally, I often prefer to start with the documents that are available in the story, but there are times when—if I know there are documents that are deep enough to document the background of the story––it might feel right to start with the stories of what happened. So, in terms of trying to establish your own personal writing or reporting voice, one style would definitely be that of bringing out the voices of people you have met in your research.

Who You Reach Out to Is Part of Who You Are

Taking the time to specifically reach out to new communities for news coverage can help grow your audience. That's because as you weave together a more complete picture of your community of coverage, the more people in your community want to learn about themselves.

As you are beginning to consider a project around investigating an important issue or cultural trend in your area, you can start by building a database of social media pages of the issues that you're looking into. Make a note of the people who administer those pages and reach out to them; make it a point to keep up with their social media for events those organizations and people are organizing. Keeping a tight connection to the doers in your community of coverage is one of the most important ways to stay on top of news.

There is a lot of variability in terms of how conscientious social media administrators are when journalists ask for information. But nevertheless, that's a place to start.

One last thing: When you are just beginning as a reporter or writer, be aware that social media platforms such as Facebook tend to show their users things they think those users want to see rather than interesting new things, at times. So try to make it a point to break out of the social media bubbles when you're learning about new people and things within your communities of interest and expertise.

Nurturing Your Zone

On a personal note, in the work I have done producing the news at a small community radio station, we can never really beat out all of the big professional radio stations. That's why our five o'clock news broadcast is a community engagement machine, built around everyday people in our local communities running projects to make the world a better place. Most nights of the week, we bring in at least one live guest who is a grassroots community organizer specializing in one issue after another, from kids to solar power to police accountability.

What never ceases to amaze me is that more and more dedicated and compelling local community groups are having a hard time getting media access because there are fewer and fewer reporters covering important regular beats, including neighborhood news and the environment.

A lot of people rely on social media to get the word out for their political events, but the shortcoming of that is most platforms like Facebook are not designed to help you reach out to new audiences.

So, where it can be possible to be heard on the television or radio station, local people with an important project or message always need producers and programmers who can provide access to the airwaves.

Trolls Suck

It is unfortunately true that in this modern age, unbalanced individuals use social media and other digital tools as weapons to harass and demean. If at times it seems that your appeals for information or interviews are going unaddressed, the people you are trying to reach might be experiencing online harassment that is driving them away from their own social media.

How do you decide when you have made too many interview queries? For myself, I limit interview requests and things of that nature to two emails and two phone calls. When I am trying to get an interview about something, I often send my interviewee (in advance) a list of three questions that I will ask. I do the same thing when I am setting up live interviews on the nightly news with grassroots community members who are not accustomed to being on the radio. I avoid this with elected officials and government bureaucrats though.

Control Versus Collaboration

As a journalist, you should never allow the people you are covering to control your process of creating a piece of journalism and broadcasting it. But that can be a fine line, because when you are covering a dangerous situation, such as violence connected to organized crime, your sources might not want to cooperate with you if they do not trust you to tell their story fairly. Part of developing your voice as a journalist can be a matter of whose side you are on when it comes to struggles that rock your community of coverage.

Think about items like this in advance, before they happen. It may seem impossible, but it's not; just consciously stop and give a thought to what impact your story might have on all of the people you met while you were investigating it. In fact, you should be doing that anyway. Right?

On the other hand, there may be a time when an organization you respect and trust may have some statistical data regarding an important issue that they do not know what to do with; you on the other hand, love playing with data, but you don't have any. If you are in this sort of situation, create at least the most basic agreement at the start regarding who has the right to publish what information on the Internet, under what circumstances and at what time. This is called a "memo of understanding."

Physical Aspects of Voice

While you dream of your future life as a Pulitzer Prize-winning genius, you're probably not thinking that much about the actual sound of your voice or the way you hold your face when you're talking. The truth is that there's a little bit of show business mixed in with broadcast journalism and podcasting.

This is another piece of how you present yourself to the world: Are you crisply organized? Or conversational and jokey? Are you reaching for a deep, authoritative feel? Or a voice that is more personal, touching on more personal subjects? Just as it is worthwhile to stop and think about your voice, it's worth it to think about the physical aspects of your voice—and your face, if you're interested in video—and take a deliberate approach to creating a digital interface with the world.

Also, keep in mind that the sounds you include in your podcast can shape your on-air identity as much as the words. The daily syndicated news, music, and public affairs show *Hard Knock Radio* is produced by Davey D at the Pacifica Studios in Oakland, California. Davey does a number of important interviews outdoors on the sidewalk near busy streets, with field recorders; the surrounding environment gets a voice in his report. That audio atmosphere gives listeners a sense of being in a conversation with interesting people in our own neighborhood.

That approach does not work for everything, but it is worth trying. If you are just starting out producing audio or video pieces, it may feel awkward. The only way to work on your voice is to voice things. You have to get out there and do it. It really is a good idea to get used to the sound of your own voice. The more you listen to your own broadcasts, the more you can work to change aspects of your voice or delivery that you do not like.

Keep It Going

How to keep a complex reporting project going is actually one of the most important things to think about in advance; it's much harder than it seems. It's the other aspect of your voice: creating episodes, one after another, that use the same production values, the same music and voices, so that listeners know exactly what it is before they're told. It might be about commercial cooking operations, or political street demonstrations, or lectures by important people—a big part of establishing your voice as a journalist is just being there week after week. If you are planning a new syndicated media project such as a podcast, your choice of theme music might be crucial.

It's never a bad idea to start out by looking for a role model—someone or something with a style or substance that resonates for you and your own digital broadcast project. Think about that person or project; what is it that they do that makes them so successful? What tools do they use? What solutions are they offering to their audience? Can you see yourself presenting your big idea in a way that feels successful for you?

The next step will seem boring to some people: Write out a ten-page script of your podcast. Let yourself loose on the page to build your show word by word and introduce the elements that are comprising your broadcast, whether they be video clips or audio clips or a slideshow.

EXERCISES

- Do a little research and find your three favorite personalities on the Internet. Why do you like them? What kinds of platforms do they use? How would you characterize their messages? Now do a little more research and find your three least favorite personalities on the Internet. What do you dislike about them? What seems to make them popular in their markets? What kind of guests do they have?

- Do a little research and find three guests you would be interested in interviewing for broadcast about the topic of your choice. For each guest, brainstorm ten questions you would ask during the interview.

- Take a few of the questions you just brainstormed for potential guests and work them into a commentary—whether it's written out or dictated into an audio recorder or phone camera. Then take that and convert it into a five to seven-minute broadcast. Listen to it a few times and decide what you might choose to change about your delivery. Then do it all again with a different topic until you feel ready to produce an entire show for yourself.

CHECK IT OUT!

One of the early investigative reporters in the U.S. was Nellie Bly, who today is considered the originator of a form of investigative journalism known as "experiential" reporting, which simply means doing something, then writing about your own experience of how it went and what insights you gained in doing it. In 1887, Bly, who wrote for the *New York World*, went undercover at an insane asylum to report about its conditions by experiencing them herself. After several days, she was released and wrote one of the first-ever media exposés in the U.S., "Ten Days in a Madhouse," which resulted in better funding for mental facilities in New York. Bly is most famous for traveling around the world in a record 72 days, which was inspired by *Around the World in 80 Days*, the novel by Jules Verne. Today, journalists use experiential reporting as a versatile storytelling tool: travel writing, writing about cooking, and—of course—memoirs are all framed this way. Almost any kind of experience could make an interesting story, whether it's serious or funny or simply informational.

Fight Cyberstalkers with Community

A word on cyberstalking and bullying. As a journalist, there may come a day when you do something or don't do something that makes you the target of anonymous cyberbullies, or what I call the Anonymous Cyberbully Goon Squad. This happened to me a couple of years ago in connection to a nonprofit board of directors that I served on.

I was targeted by anonymous cyberstalkers who tried to damage my reputation among my professional colleagues in the media in the town where I live and work. What I learned was that the only thing that helped me was the community that I had built around me. That's in spite of embarrassment, worry over how it would affect my family and coworkers, and anger that anyone would make completely fabricated attacks against me without identifying themselves. Because I have a track record in my work and my community commitment, people were able to look at these baseless accusations and see them for what they were.

I was also lucky because, as a journalist, I have a large body of work on the Internet that pushed links to the attack website off of the first page of searches for my name. The Anonymous Cyberbully Goon Squad's harassment website is still up, even today, even though the bullies that put them there have long since abandoned them. Companies charge several hundred dollars to "scrub" these attacks against you from the top of your Internet searches, but they can almost never really get rid of them completely.

When this happens to you, it can be devastating, emotionally and professionally. My advice is to reach out to the people who know you best and just keep building a positive community around your work, whatever it may be. All of my own personal fantasies of revenge against the people that I thought made these attacks against me came to nothing, by the way, which means I completely played into their petty, destructive little hands. If this happens to you, do not be like me and waste time with fantasies of revenge. Circle the wagons of your community, recommit yourself to positivity, and forge ahead.

STORY IDEA
"Vox Pop"

Speaking of voices, one of the most loved forms of reporting is called a "vox pop," in Latin known as a *vox populi*, or "voice of the people." You literally come up with one question and ask a whole bunch of people the same thing, then report on their responses. These can be done using video, audio recordings, or written interviews.

Taking this idea to an extreme, decades ago a reporter named Studs Terkel took it as his life's work to interview everyday people about their jobs. From a teenager at a switchboard for the phone company to garbage collectors and more, Terkel captured true voices seldom heard in our major media, eventually creating radio pieces and publishing books of his interviews. Can you think of people in your community whose voices are seldom heard?

CHAPTER 10

PLATFORMS: BUILDING YOUR PLACE IN THE JOURNALISM WORLD

"Journalism without a moral position is impossible. Every journalist is a moralist. It's absolutely unavoidable. A journalist is someone who looks at the world and the way it works, someone who takes a close look at things every day and reports what she sees, someone who represents the world, the event, for others. She cannot do her work without judging what she sees."

—Marguerite Duras, *Outside: Selected Writings*

I n this chapter, you will learn the meaning of digital platform, and you will begin to choose where you will build your digital presence to maximize your message.

You've learned how to spot whether an issue is newsworthy, how to gather information about the issue, and how to arrange that information. Excellent! Now it's time to figure out where on the Internet you want to present all your stuff. What kind of platform do you need?

YOU WILL LEARN:

- Don't get carried away with all the things you want your website to do—you'll find audiences don't care how cool you think it is; they just want it to load faster.

- Photography, videos, writing—it's your job to find the best platforms that showcase all of your media skills.

- Get ready to make a few mistakes; keep in mind the very first recording (or five?) you make might not be the best. That's because we learn by doing.

What is a media platform? A platform is literally like a digital shelf where you store your words and pictures and videos and audio so that other people—your audience, including your mom—can come over and consume it. They might even share it with their friends. Think about whatever form your journalism takes: photography? Written stories? Video? All of that? Are you using your own site? Are you using a page on Facebook? Are you building out a Twitter account for a specific event or project?

Now think about when they are loaded onto the Internet, each website your mom visits to take in every one of your media posts because she doesn't want to miss a single one. Those websites are each a platform. Sometimes you will have your digital content on multiple platforms, and you want people to share them all around for each one of those platforms.

If your strategy is to become an independent journalist, if you hope to get paid by others, you will still need a media platform of your own to show off what you can do. Take the time to practice your due diligence in finding out the best platforms for each one of your media skills. Take the time to look up whether these platforms are compatible with each other and whether they have a history of changing their operations suddenly. This is crucial because key platforms, over time, change ownership or go out of business; if you pick the wrong basket for your eggs, sometimes you can lose out.

A good place to start in figuring out what kind of digital platform you need for your reporting is to list, for yourself, the kinds of media you want to publish––audio, video, text, photographs, or what have you.

Take five minutes and research the most used platforms for each one of those forms of media (use the five-point search method you learned in Chapter 4: Information Gathering). What are you coming up with? Make a detailed list of your media publishing needs; include any potential costs, including server space for a website and any further equipment you might need. Do they cost money?

Building Your Own

When you are in the position of having to build your own media platform to get your message out, that means you have to do the same thing that William Randolph Hearst and S.I. Newhouse, Sr., did. You have to become your own media mogul, and that's kind of a big deal. Allow me to suggest your very first lesson: don't get carried away. This is another topic where many books have been written about the details.

My goal here is just to plant a few ideas for your beginning stages of organization. Also, I want to give you a few warnings on things not to do. At the newspaper where I'd worked for many years, we spent two years developing a new website. It was going to be perfect, with responsive design, and lots of pictures, and movies and sound and yada, yada, yada. At last, when the website was built, it was all that and more; but just to upload one article took about twenty minutes.

With website development, spending too much money by getting yourself in too deep with custom-built applications and functions is one of the biggest dangers to success. There are quite a few examples of fancy news websites that start out with a splash, then fade away under their own weight in too many bells and whistles and a lack of advertising sales. In creating your street journalism digital platform, you really can make a big impact in your own way as long as you are strategic and organized.

One of my favorite blogs involved three anonymous female journalists who analyzed the inner workings of Seattle politics and culture using short-form writing, tweets, GIFs, and small animal photos. Somehow the formula allows for hilarious and focused, pointed commentary on what would otherwise be boring points of city policy. Their spontaneous drinking games for anyone watching city or county council meetings from home via live stream are fucking hilarious.

Bottom line, my advice is: Don't get carried away with your means of production. As you're thinking about the message you have for the world, you're also thinking about what that message will look like on a digital page. Set boundaries for yourself in terms of bells and whistles and what kind of workload each story should require in uploading to your new zone.

Simple is beautiful. Having said that, now you need to choose what kind of media you realistically produce, and my advice is for each person involved to stick with one medium at first until you get the lay of the land; then shake it up if you are so moved.

Get a Handle on Your Equipment

Whatever platform you use, the tools you need to fill it with content are almost certainly going to be electronic toys of one kind or another. Video cameras, handheld audio field recorders, smart phones, computer tablets, laptops, and PCs with big hardware towers-- you are going to need equipment to actually build out whichever platforms you choose.

I recently met a man who does an entire YouTube video blog with just his phone. He is energetic, with bright clothing and a charming mohawk haircut, and every film he makes is a selfie of himself talking to people on the street, asking them questions and recording their responses (this is called a "vox pop" format, meaning "voice of the people")--and it's pretty much the most basic, efficient system imaginable for creating a media presence:

- You've got your media platform--YouTube;
- your means of production--a smartphone;
- and your content--this fun man interviewing people on the street.

The production process involves just creating the selfie video and uploading it on the spot. It's almost elegant in its simplicity.

The Tools You Need

To get the ball rolling on figuring out your news platform, start by figuring out what you wish you had in terms of tools to cover your stories the way you want to. A little time researching the news innovations of other people is easy-peasy-lemon-squeezy; simply go online to look up keywords relating to what you're trying to figure out. If you are working on a single, one-time project, you can experiment by picking one out of the endless stream of new news platforms to build it on.

A caution I would make to you is—again—beware of investing a lot of time in a special project on a platform that might itself go bankrupt or become obsolete, like Flip cameras. Remember Flip cameras? I didn't think so. Similarly, I would warn you to beware of platforms that will try to make you pay later for the space where your material is being stored; you don't want to be in a ransom situation with a website over your entire collection of photographs that you've taken in the past year, just to take one example.

Content that Builds Community

Most of the time, when people think about successful media, they are thinking about hard-hitting issues and reporting that digs at the facts. Don't forget though, some of the best reporting doesn't take things apart—sometimes it builds up what is beautiful and nurtures everyday people in specific ways.

Here are a few ideas about reporting projects that build community:

Create an oral history project

No matter what area you are interested in, there must be someone, somewhere who started it. There must be somebody who owns important memorabilia, or who is descended from an influential leader, or who wrote a big book about your town. One of the most enjoyable projects you can ever do with a media outlet is invite people into shared stories about important times in history within your area of interest.

Sometimes the people you invited in are really old, sometimes they're really young. One thing that surprises me is how many people in your listening audience really do want to hear these stories you have gathered. As far as outreach projects built around community partnerships, you could strategically build a program with an organization where young volunteers use digital equipment to interview older generations about a variety of topics, with the final interviews all being housed on the website of that nonprofit organization.

Create an obituary section

For many people, obituaries are a relic of the past. Originally intended as small articles in newspapers about people who've just passed away, in the digital age they've become electric stories that can capture the intimate character of lost loved ones that are shared out on social media. Today, simple obituaries published on just about any website can serve as a mourning spot for family and friends who miss the person memorialized on that page. In some cases, mourners return to a page year after year to leave respects and remembrances; I do it myself.

Youth opportunities

One of the most wonderful investments that you could make as a media outlet in building community partnerships is to offer internships to local youth. You cannot do this unless you have an absolutely safe environment to do it in, and dedicated and skilled people to supervise, not to mention compliance with all local state and federal laws regarding licensing.

The most important thing about institutionalizing youth opportunities within your emerging street journalism project is that over time, you are building a new generation of journalists from the ground up. This is crucial because over the past twenty years and more, massive cuts to school funding have led to the elimination of many high school journalism programs and other writing opportunities for kids.

It is just my personal experience as a community media manager that a small, consistent stream of young people start out in small media boiler rooms and then go on to national jobs, graduate school, or law school, for whatever reason. There is something about volunteering in a newsroom that builds up the intellectual muscles of many people.

Your own community outreach project

If you are dreaming of a local news outlet online, you can maximize that dream with real face time with real people in your community of interest, offline. It is simply my experience that putting the two together is more than the sum of its parts.

My advice is to draft a two-year plan for how you are going to conduct community outreach in your media project. Start with choosing a platform––some kind of digital platform––where you will be organizing your documents and emails and other basic contact information on. You also need some kind of digital platform to publicize your work and interact with your community. Whether it is your own website or blog, or a dedicated multimedia social media page cluster, have a timeline on when it's going to be ready and what kind of interactive projects and appeals you are going to put out there.

A simple outreach project would be something as simple as working with a local café owner to call a Saturday morning "no host" breakfast at the café for fans of your project or issue; that kind of event is a win-win because you support the local, small business and also get to meet your own online community that you seldom see. I, personally, am a big fan of modest steps, especially if they are simply plotted out on a calendar with a timeline and phone numbers written by it.

Filling Up Your Platform with Content

It can take you months, even longer maybe, to get your new website or social media cloud set up so that you can begin loading your content onto it. You should spend that time stockpiling about three months' worth of content, like a squirrel planning for the winter. You've already chosen the outline for exactly what kind of articles you want to be loading onto your platforms and at what time of the week or month you want to publish. Now you've got your systems in gear and you're moving forward. Nice!

Regular Production

Make a schedule for what you need to get done throughout the month to make sure that your media gets distributed through your platforms—that's called a production schedule. Production is the process of putting your content into distribution, including the writing, taking pictures, pasting them up on the page, uploading items to the Internet, and then reposting those items that have been uploaded so that they get distributed to the maximum number of audience members.

As you look at what platforms you plan to use in publishing your content, you're taking into account your content inventory and how to follow the easiest process to pull each entire thing together. This can actually be very fun—especially if you're the kind of person who likes organizing things.

Great Social Media

If you are just coming to the concept of building community around social media platforms, the first thing you should know about is Search Engine Optimization (SEO). When you look at a page on a website, you see certain words that are headlines and other words under photographs that are called photo captions. These groups of words and others are actually like invisible Internet magnets that draw people who are searching online using these same specific words.

So, it's critical to understand that what you're doing first is coming up with clumps of words to describe what you're posting on your Internet pages so that those words will attract other people searching for the same things. Start with that base of knowledge.

You don't have to be a certain type of person to win a lot of followers on social media. The key is to know what your goals are, then come up with a plan that might take you there.

Create Your Social Media Style

This is one of the strange areas of social media that can have a big impact on whether a given project finds its audience or not. As you look at the different kinds of social media platforms––Facebook, Twitter, YouTube, whichever of the other ones you may prefer–– you can see they're not all created equal. That's in part because of constraints over length of the message, whether there is audio, whether there is video, and a variety of other factors.

But, depending on what your project involves, planning in advance for a few consistent, defining artistic features would help you literally brand the project but also have a little fun. You could use touches such as: audio interviews conducted in urban environments including street corners; graphics that incorporate one special color that you particularly prefer with your projects; any sort of logo or graphic or special name that you associate with your work; if you are an artist or artisan, you would use photographs of yourself demonstrating your work.

In creating their own social media style, remarkable social media practitioners have made their mark in terms of using different kinds of language, creating videos using unique film styles, and recording podcasts with hilarious sound effects. All of these things are part of creating your own style.

Protect Your Own Name

If you are a street journalist who is just starting out and creating a social media presence that you can use to publicize your media platforms, consider taking out accounts preserving your own project name in a variety of media platforms, even if you do not intend to publish on them; that's so that you can control your own name which you are doing business by elsewhere.

My sweetheart tried to start a Twitter account in the name of his entertainment company, but when he tried to register it, his own name was already taken by what looked like a robot account based in Arizona. You never could get any response from the account holder, who never did tweet anything.

Consider creating accounts even on popular platforms that you do not intend to use, especially if they're free of charge.

Linking It Up

As you think about building your own digital media platform, look at how other people's media links look on whichever is your target social media. Do the posts look pretty? Are the links from the website opening up into big windows with a photograph and headline and a subtext? Or are they opening into small text boxes with no images and just a few words? As you are distributing your important content, try to make sure the postings you make on social media look inviting.

Once you choose which platforms you will use for your reporting, find all of the ways you can to connect them together—but try to avoid setting them up so that they all publish the same thing at the same time. Go ahead and connect perhaps two or three platforms together to carry the same posts, but not everything you have, because that starts to seem like spam.

When you see that a platform you're using is rolling out an experimental project, definitely sign on and check it out. Play with these opportunities when you can and encourage your friends to do it too. Keep in mind the very first take on whatever it is might not be the best. But you can only learn by doing, so get ready to make some mistakes.

Plan Your "Opening"

Because there is a lot of work involved in launching a media outlet, you can make it easier on yourself by planning your time efficiently. If you start out with a very detailed plan, you'll have more control over how the entire thing rolls out.

An important aspect of publishing is making a good first impression by weaving in participation by respected people in your field. If you can plan out the next six months' worth of publishing projects, you can take that same opportunity to add to each one some kind of an outreach project and bring in a community or individual influencer for some sort of special event.

Make it a point to keep pulling in these influencers in addition to the everyday people coming to your events.

As you are preparing for the opening of your media platforms, take the time to be deliberate about organizations and businesses who are also part of the community you are serving. You could create a spreadsheet with the names and contact information of your supporters and a separate section for business and nonprofit organizations.

Another way to create this spreadsheet is to simply track all of the individuals that you interview and publish on your media outlet to make sure that you keep connected to them in the future. When you take the time to build stronger relationships to the people that you have interviewed within your area of expertise, you are building relationships that might last for years, even decades to come.

This is an important part of how you do your job. It includes your ability to listen to what your community connections have to say about the issues, and it also gives you the opportunity to tell their expertise on a breaking news situation or when you're covering an issue that you've stumbled upon as you're walking down the street.

Building on Positivity

Building your community is more like growing a garden, less like going shopping at the grocery store. If you are considering creating a social media plan for an outlet or project, you should plan ahead at least six months.

That's why you should try to avoid the situation where you're an asshole on your own social media and then you're forced to do damage control. The better strategy is just to avoid being unfairly harsh against your colleagues on your social media. That's especially true if you ever think you'll use your social media to help raise funds for an important project of yours.

When it's one of those handful of times when you have to raise a gigantic fundraising goal within the next seven days, it is too late to create an entire social media platform to serve your purposes in such a short period.

Consider creating a 90-day social media improvement plan for your immediate project. You can cultivate the seeds of relationships with individual people and with organizations to see if they will grow.

When it comes to that new social media account, keep everything in it positive. Use it to praise other peers also connected to the project. Evaluate your effectiveness in growing a network around your campaign. If you can grow your networks even modestly, it makes every time you have to raise money a little easier.

Fundraising

Which brings us to the biggest avenues for making money from news platforms, for grassroots people anyway: Online crowdfunding platforms and old-fashioned membership drives allow you to lay out your funding plan with an appeal online and try to raise money to make it happen. Funding platforms seem to change over time, but chances are you still need to learn how to make a money pitch.

Don't feel uncomfortable about it—it's not that you're begging to strangers for money, it's that you're offering people of integrity an opportunity to invest in a meaningful activity that could change the world for the better. You'd be surprised at how many people are just looking for a way to put their money in a place where it can do some good.

Do not fall into the trap of seeing a number of successful online money campaigns and then assuming they must be easy to do right. Make it your business to scrutinize every successful Kickstarter in your immediate communities. See how much money the campaign asked for and establish a timeline for how much money came in.

Take a moment to scrutinize the names of people thanked for making a contribution. Are they people you know? Successful online fundraising appeals do not happen by accident. Figure out which of these people are the ones that make them successful.

Make a Simple Pitch

No matter how you plan to pay for your street journalism, the fact is you'll have to start with a simple pitch. Sometimes it can be difficult to keep your mouth from running on and on, especially when you're talking to strangers. But when you're trying to sell your big idea to someone who might seem intimidating for whatever reason, keeping your sentences brief and allowing there to be silence can be impressive.

The most important thing about making a pitch is to have your information organized in your mind; be ready to rank items in order of importance while you are thinking on your feet. Also take a moment to realize that in some cases, people that you are trying to pitch your big idea to are looking for big ideas worth investing in. Just like you, they're probably casting a wide net to draw in the people that they want to build relationships with.

One thing I consistently find when it comes to making a pitch, especially if it's a financial pitch (including at a membership drive) is that if you don't ask for the big amounts of money, you almost certainly will not get them. So, as you're writing an outline of how you're going to make your pitch, be completely clear about what you're asking for. Ask for a little bit more than what you actually really expect to get.

Here Are a Few Tips on Writing a Good Pitch:

- Keep it positive. Disaster response aside, it's hard to build a good pitch from a negative point of view. It is my experience that the best frame for a fundraising event is to build it around some sort of solution to a difficult problem. In any event, even though you might have content that's really compelling, if it's negative, people just won't want to give money.
- Build excitement. You will find during a really connected fundraising process, such as a live broadcast auction or other event, that when some people start to pledge money it can turn into a domino effect of other people wanting to contribute money. This is where you use thank you gifts and other special rewards for people who, quote, "call now."
- Sometimes it's helpful in your fundraising efforts to be specific about how the money will be spent, i.e. for a new website, a phone system, or for a special journalistic trip or project.
- Debate exists in fundraising circles about whether it's better to offer people a thank you gift for their contribution or whether it's better to focus on signing people up for regular contributions, such as memberships. Pay attention to this debate.

Create a Special Event

Some media outlets host annual public social events as a combination of fundraisers and celebration for their supporters. For a nonprofit media outlet, a signature event could be an annual Halloween party, or a banquet, or an annual meeting. If you're thinking about creating an annual event as an additional revenue stream for your street journalism organization, a common best practice for projects like this is to include a public service component, such as a volunteer award or college scholarships. You could even do both. Another best practice for sit-down events is to have a keynote speaker articulate in the subject area of your coverage. The keynote speaker can generate a call to action that might be needed in your area of expertise and can bring important ideas from the outside world into your local community, where perhaps your conversations need to be broader.

The third value of having a keynote speaker is they might draw a lot of people to your event—that's if you choose one who is compelling to people within your community of interest. When you're just starting out and creating an annual event, if you do choose the keynote speaker format, consider making a lasting relationship with the people that you have invited to do that over the years.

Again, that's called building community around your work. If you bring an influential keynote speaker to your annual event, you should be connecting your social media to theirs. If you spend a little time thinking about it in advance, you might be able to feed many birds with one hand.

EXERCISES

- Make a laundry list of ten upcoming community events that your media outlet's listeners would be interested in hearing about or attending. If you are finding these events on your social media, take a moment to tag or retweet or like these events as you go as well. See yourself as building an extended web of media contacts with people in your own community.

- Consider taking some sort of digital recording device with you and attending the event. Introduce yourself to people there and try to get brief interviews with several people about their take on what's going on with the biggest issues of the day––a vox pop. You could also take the opportunity to record your own voiceover about what is taking place around you. It should go without saying that you would do that in such a way as to not disturb the scene that might be unfolding.

- Create a one-hour-a-week plan to improve your street journalism project's reach using social media. Start to build community around your social media by identifying a dozen colleagues and supporters in your immediate online networks, whatever those may be. The idea is to just spend one hour per week focusing on a systematic plan to build listenership of your broadcast.

CHECK IT OUT!

Live streaming is a journalistic tool that involves broadcasting an event live, as it happens, using some kind of digital equipment, such as a smartphone or tablet computer. (When you take the broadcast and record it as it airs for re-watching later, that is a webcast.) German reporter Paul Ronzheimer of the *Bild* newspaper, reporting in 2015 as he traveled across the Middle East alongside Syrian refugees, used the Periscope app to live stream interviews with Syrian refugees who were trying to reach Germany. The live connection between refugees and the outside world—especially families with children—created a uniquely personal and touching information flow.

Periscope

TECHNIQUE

Basic Equipment Tips

When it comes to equipment, I've got good news and bad news. The good news is there are always going to be perfectly fine toys for making pictures and video and for live streaming ducklings crossing the street. The bad news is there will always be a new gadget that just came out that revolutionizes journalism, blah, blah, blah.

This is my advice on equipment:

- Use equipment to bring to the surface the voices that are not being heard--this is where street journalists have an advantage, because you live outside the bubble that the rest of the media is trapped in.

- Find where the voices are, then use the equipment to weave the voices into your work.

- When it comes to your work as a street journalist, choose your equipment like you choose your footwear--you like it nice? Get nice. You like it to take you places? Get it sturdier.

- There is too much equipment in this world; if you have equipment that fails to bring in voices, leave it by the side of the road.

- Always have a backup.

- Once you start figuring out what you love most, stick with equipment that's tried and true--never go for the newest, biggest thing unless someone else is paying for it.

- Most important of all is energy, energy, energy. Are all your devices charged? Do you have spare batteries or energy booster packs? Energy, energy, energy.

STORY IDEA

Make a Map

If your interests include anything relating to geography, figure out some kind of digital project with GPS and maps. I stumbled on the idea of making "ghost maps" on gentrification several years ago because I was in my city's history archive and they have a copy of the telephone book from 1956. Back then, not only did the telephone book have people's addresses and phone numbers, but they also listed all the individual residents that lived along the streets, in order.

When I plugged every one of those addresses into a Google map, suddenly you could see what exists today in places where there used to be homes and vibrant businesses. In many cases, what exists now is a freeway overpass or an empty lot. The only data I had to obtain for that project was old addresses out of a phone book, but the ghost maps showed just what the old residents had lost over the generations.

CHAPTER 11

CONCLUSION

"Independent media can go to where the silence is and break the sound barrier, doing what the corporate networks refuse to do."

—Amy Goodman, *Democracy Now!*

I want to end our conversation about street journalism by taking the most essential tips I outlined for you here and showing how I personally used them in one of the most important stories I ever covered: the police killing of Aaron Campbell , an unarmed African-American resident of Portland who fell into a mental health crisis at his home in 2010. Mr. Campbell's death always stands out because of the ways his situation could have gone right but didn't. This beloved young man died because of a bureaucratic fuckup that put his life on the line and, racism. As a reporter, this story called me to continually stretch past my limitations in ways few other assignments have. It's the best possible example of why independent community journalism can be a matter of life or death and how local reporters on the spot can be crucial in showing the world what's happening now.

If you are following along with your street journalism cookbook, we are looking at our list of ingredients and checking what they actually look like when we cook with them:

- Is This a Story?
- How Will You Tell It?
- Solutions Journalism
- Fake News, Brain Farts, and Crap Detectors
- Information Gathering
- Interviewing Tips
- Pulling It All Together and Telling the Story
- Fact-checking
- What Is Investigative Reporting?

- Platforms: Building Your Place in the Journalism World

Let's get started.

Is This a Story?

My hometown of Portland, Oregon, is misleading. It looks green and friendly, but in fact it has a well-documented history of racist violence, just as the state itself does. The Portland Police Bureau has spent years fighting off resident-led attempts to establish independent police review, and the efforts all end up in the toilet. Meanwhile, Portland (like every city in the U.S., but surprisingly more so than many) has an established history of police harassment of African-American residents. By the time I sat at my desk at the *Skanner* newspaper office late on a Friday afternoon in January of 2010, I was thinking about going home for the weekend. Suddenly, a friend called and asked if I had any information about a police shooting. Then a rush of emails had me glued to the computer: The police had shot and killed a young black man named Aaron Campbell. Over the next two hours, more information trickled out of city bureaus and sources calling with news tips. The man was in a mental health crisis because his beloved brother died at the hospital of a congenital heart problem earlier that day. Mr. Campbell's mother had lost all of her sons, unexpectedly, within hours of each other.

The fact is, for many newsrooms, the shooting of a young black man almost anywhere in America during the year 2010 would not be considered particularly newsworthy. But the African-American newspaper where I worked had covered police-involved shootings and incidents for generations; for us it was a big deal, no question about it. The police accountability aspect made it clearly a civil rights story, which meant I had to pay attention to specific details likely to impact the story's outcome: past legal cases of the police bureau, including monetary payouts triggered by lawsuits and grievances in similar situations to this one; statistics about the people most often stopped and charged with crimes; whether or not there was a history of criticism of policy or leadership on civil rights issues; and more.

How Will You Tell It?

I decided to gather the information that a federal civil rights investigator would if they were looking into a constitutional violation around this incident, essentially: Is there a history of fatal shootings by law enforcement in the city? If so, who is killed most often? Sitting down to piece together what happened during Mr. Campbell's shooting, it was clear that there were several ways this story could be told——keeping in mind that all stories are about people, doing something, for a reason, right? It seems simple, but as a journalist, the ways you choose to frame the information you are presenting can have far-reaching consequences; you should stop and think about that as you frame your story. When there is a lot of emotionally charged information on the table, it's best to stick with the basics: What actually happened? And what factors are in play during this situation?

As I watched the first stories appear about Mr. Campbell's shooting, most went like this: A Portland Police officer fatally shot an armed black man in a tense standoff at an apartment building. The next batch of stories went like this: A Portland Police officer fatally shot a man he believed to be armed after a tense standoff at an apartment building. My own take on the facts was that the police bureau's crisis negotiator had talked Mr. Campbell out of his apartment before other officers shot, sent an attack dog, and tasered Mr. Campbell all at the same time.

"Solutions Journalism"

Simply knowing that the police had shot and killed an African-American man in a mental health crisis, and that news of the events was still rolling out, told me a few things as a small independent journalist. One, it meant that there would probably be so much fear-based coverage of the horrifying details of what happened that media consumers would start turning away from the story. To me, that meant that *The Skanner* should fill the gap left by bigger media by focusing on the grassroots response to the tragedy and give space to creative people organizing on the issue––what we described earlier in this book as "solutions journalism." Writing about the response to a tragedy can give you the opportunity to uplift the work of everyday people and also help fight against the kind of general hopelessness that social media seems to incubate. A general "solutions journalism" approach to this issue could include: follow-up interviews with people fundraising to support the family in some way, such as paying for attorneys or funeral expenses; a look at organizations that support families of murder victims and what they do, profiling the work of a civil rights law first that takes on cases like this, or any institution that supports families of victims in fatal police shootings; and investigative scrutiny of any report or process or verdict that comes of the tragic incident you are covering.

Information Gathering

When the police fatally shoot someone, it is often considered to be on a different level than street shootings involving civilians.

That's because when law enforcement takes a life, they are being paid with taxpayer dollars, and the act itself represents, for many people, government-sanctioned killing without the benefit of court or independent review. That's why when this kind of event happens, it can sometimes draw hundreds or thousands of people into the streets, or a harsh media spotlight into municipal policies and practices. Within hours of Mr. Campbell's fatal shooting, the police bureau started issuing gigantic press releases and free police reports and transcripts that they normally would charge $10 per page for, detailing the official bureau position on what their officers had done and why. For me, these moments become a journalistic Easter egg hunt where the seeker looks for inconsistencies and contradictions in the government's version of events. The minute I found out what happened to Mr. Campbell, I stopped crying and wiped off my nose with the back of my hand and opened a computer browser just on the police bureau to make sure I wouldn't miss any document dumps. Then I did the same thing with the county district attorney website, where they post grand jury announcements on big cases.

Interviewing Tips

On finding sources: Go straight to the heart of impacted communities for information first, not second; this will have a fundamental impact on how you frame the story. I would like to stop here and make a strong point: Take control of your own journalistic process with an informed approach on how your mind works. Remember the "fake news" chapter where we talked about cognitive biases, especially "confirmation bias?" Your fundamental understanding of a situation will almost certainly be impacted on who you speak to first in your investigation process. In the case of Mr. Campbell's killing, I consciously arranged to speak with the family member before talking to the police bureau. In my work, generally, I prefer to cultivate the frame of everyday people experiencing large institutions rather than the other way around, which is the more common frame for general news coverage. Hours after the shooting, a longtime community contact of mine put me in touch with a relative of Mr. Campbell who was close to the situation; that person described the events running up to the police confrontation. The relative did not want to be named but agreed to be quoted as a balance to the police's statements about what happened and why. The family member agreed to forward details on any fundraising efforts or any other family requests or needs. I expressed condolences for their loss.

Pulling It All Together and Telling the Story

Right here, in the first 24 hours of a big breaking story, is the place where as a journalist, you have to help readers figure out "what is truth" in a given situation, so let's take a few moments to unpack this point. How do you decide "who's telling the truth?" Or is that even the right question to ask——why not instead just weigh out equal measures of facts as if all sides might be right? In this particular story, I knew this would be a key step. That's because so much of the time in similar cases, the police account and witness accounts differ, but the law enforcement official always walks away with their job while more local residents become more afraid of walking down the street or taking public transit. We've seen this for years, and it's a tough nut to crack. So, in preparing this report, I wanted to make an extra effort at fairness and accuracy because police shootings are a matter of life and death.

In my years of experience covering city government, a police report that says a law enforcement officer had no choice in shooting to kill a black man who had no firearm in his hand is often debatable. But the fact that a sentence or two in a police report might say the officer feared for his life tends to give it the credibility of fact, even if it isn't true. As I worked on my first and second reports on Mr. Campbell's death, I noted the official police story that officers thought he had a gun and could hurt them––even though officers were theoretically there to keep Mr. Campbell from hurting himself. Using my experience in covering similar cases, I suspected that the police bureau might later reveal that Mr. Campbell was not holding a weapon; I was right––after he was killed, Mr. Campbell's handgun was found stored in a closet in his apartment. His cousin described how much Mr. Campbell loved his brother, who had died that morning after fighting off heart disease for years. Mr. Campbell was so depressed over the death that family members worried he might take his own life. One relative called police and requested a "welfare check" to make sure Mr. Campbell was not harming himself, and a squad car arrived at the apartment he shared with his partner and their baby. Officers learned that Mr. Campbell owned a handgun, and more squad cars were called; then they learned his girlfriend and their baby were inside with him. Now the police response bloomed into a full-fledged standoff. Early on, word was returned that the "girlfriend and baby escaped unharmed." But the standoff intensified, now with a sharpshooter and a dog team. After hours of cellphone texting, a police crisis negotiator talked Mr. Campbell out of the apartment, only to watch helplessly as Mr. Campbell was gunned down by a police sharpshooter without his command-instruction earpiece on, then attacked by a police dog as he lay dying.

Brain Farts (aka Cognitive Bias)

Much of the time, it's pretty easy to confirm what's what in a news story––you check listings and call people back to double-check details. But stories like Mr. Campbell's shooting by the police show the importance of digging at the roots of information, scrutinizing where it comes from, and testing to see if it's accurate rather than running with official sources and the first headlines that appear on the Internet.

The brain fart I grappled with in this story was attribute substitution; my gut instinct insisted that I reject the idea that these are simple situations where "all cops are bad" and stop blanket-blaming all law enforcement en masse. When I read through the reports, what stood out was the work of the crisis negotiator, who texted Mr. Campbell and created a rapport with him; when you read over the text messages in the report, you could almost imagine the two becoming friends after it all blew over. But almost as soon as Mr. Campbell backed out of the apartment with his hands over his head, other officers who hadn't been paying attention to the negotiations were allegedly caught by surprise, killing Mr. Campbell even though he was cooperating with commands.

Fact-checking: My Self-editing Checklist

For very important stories I custom build a special checklist, not just to double-check basic facts but also deeper problems that I think might get in the way of readers' ability to take in the important facts. In reporting on Mr. Campbell's case, I especially wanted to check my tone to minimize emotional language and anger; the anger made the story more confusing to follow. That's because the more plainly the facts were stated, the more shocking they became, and the more outrage I threw into the mix, the harder it was to remember who the political gatekeepers were on this issue. But even though it's not the sexiest fact in the story, I wanted to center the place where everyday people could put pressure towards a better outcome—and above all, I wanted people who read this story to be equipped to take productive action if they chose to.

Another item on the Self-editing Checklist: Accurate timelines, meaning: Get the sequence of events right. Another thing: Check with your community touchstones on a traumatic story of life and death. Ask them: What is the best way to cover this story from the point of view of communities impacted by it? What would be the worst way to cover it? What information do you think it would be great to get into the community right now? And then think about their responses. You don't have to agree with every touchstone you chose, but remember: I personally task myself with agreeing to follow what my touchstones tell me; I always have done that, and over time I have never regretted it.

Investigative Reporting

Remember when we said earlier, "the documents tell the story"? The police killing of Mr. Campbell quickly evolved from breaking news to an investigative project with hundreds of pages of police and medical examiner reports and the grand jury transcript. I read every page, with my focus specifically on procedures used by officers and timelines of the actions taken by everyone at the scene, including the police dog. I was looking for evidence of a past history of similar shootings.

In our town, there were plenty of similar cases of fatal police shootings of, specifically, men in mental health crisis situations, and also specifically black men showing or not showing hands under direct commands. I also spoke with people connected to the family and others whose loved ones were killed by police during a mental health crisis about key moments that seemed to determine the outcome in their sequence of events. I used their analysis to show the failure of the law enforcement response to mental health crisis in our local community.

Your Place in the Journalism World

The newspaper where I produced this body of work is an African-American family-owned business in one of the whitest cities in the nation, Portland, Oregon. Even though *The Skanner* is a small community media outlet, on this issue, where I had solid contacts who brought me into the story, we led the city's debate on mental health and law enforcement reform. When my boss, the owner and publisher, took his first look at my reporting, he smacked his hand down on the table and said, "If black people are in trouble, we'd better not call the police!" Within 24 hours we had an editorial up on our website warning our black readers and their loved ones away from calling law enforcement in cases where they could be shot by police officers who had been called to check on their safety. Our website almost crashed from traffic, and my boss—who loved looking at the user statistics tracked inside a special program installed for the purpose—saw that almost all of the readers could be traced to the downtown jail building, including hundreds and hundreds of hostile reader comments posted to the story on our website. The Campbell case touched off an investigation by the U.S. Department of Justice into the standards and practices of the Portland Police Bureau; it found that officers beat down mentally ill people and people of color too often. Unfortunately, the police review process set up between the USDOJ and a former mayor of Portland has since then completely collapsed. Officer Ron Frashour, who fired the fatal shot into Mr. Campbell's back with an AR-15 rifle, went on to become a lightning rod for controversy at the bureau. And the need for more street journalists to cover police accountability issues has grown.

The whole idea behind this book, *Street Journalist*, is that our communities need and deserve watchdogs to guard our public good using sharpened tools of information gathering and sharing. We should be teaching kids how to sort through different kinds of information and judge what's important. You don't need a gold-plated university certificate to be a bona fide independent reporter. My biggest hope is that you will take skills, insights, and lessons from this book and build out your own corner of the information multiverse and make it the brightest beacon of people power in the sky. Don't forget to fact-check!

CHECK IT OUT!

What is a whistleblower? In 2011, *New York Times* reporter James Risen almost went to prison over his refusal to disclose the identity of a whistleblower from inside the CIA. Risen was writing his book *The Secret History of the CIA and the Bush Administration* when a CIA fraud investigator named Jeffrey Alexander Sterling gave him information about corruption inside the spy agency. A few years earlier, Sterling—who is an African-American expert on Russia and who speaks fluent Persian, the national language of Iran—had already tried to sue his employers at the CIA for racial discrimination, but courts ruled his case would expose national secrets, so it was thrown out.

Sterling leaked to Risen the details of a plan to sell fake nuclear technology to Iran to slow down their efforts to create a bomb. Sterling was eventually unmasked by others as Risen's source, convicted under the Espionage Act, and sent to a penitentiary for three and a half years. Risen—who never did admit that Sterling was his source—won journalism's highest honor, the Pulitzer Prize.

TECHNIQUE

Better Sound and Pictures

Using electronics to get great content should be your bread and butter. Here are a few tips on capturing quality images and sound, but go ahead and read a few books on this as well:

- Are you shooting cellphone video? Turn your phone on its side before you hit the record button. That's horizontal, so the screen is widest. Don't argue, just do it. Thank you.

- Taking images such as photos and video? Avoid shooting in front of windows and bright sources of light because they turn your picture into a silhouette. Try to have light at your back, reflecting into the image you want to take.

- Ask the permission of strangers before you start live streaming because there are times when individuals can be vulnerable to real-time identification situations. This can especially impact women and kids in domestic violence situations where abusers can locate them in real time, but also people in danger from government bureaucracies.

- Focus your lens and keep the important stuff in the center.

- Frame your images by paying attention to what's in the background. You don't want to videotape the mayor's important speech about police accountability with a light fixture hovering over his head like a UFO--bad backgrounds can become distracting and ruin your important work.

The book is long on personal
advice & short on actual
useful information / tools / techniques

12/23/22

ABOUT THE AUTHOR

Lisa Loving is an award-winning journalist and media activist. As a staff member and volunteer at KBOO Community Radio in Portland, Oregon, she has trained hundreds of everyday people in the tools of independent journalism. She has reported for *Wired*, the *Oregonian*, the *New York Times* and published her first freelance article—on how to get rid of cockroaches—in the *San Jose Mercury News*. But she has spent almost her entire journalism career in community media, including a decade as news editor of the *Skanner*, an African American family-owned newspaper serving Portland and Seattle. Lisa was one of the University of Oregon Agora Center's "Front 50" regional innovators in media, and she is convinced that everyday people are—and have always been—key players in our media landscape.

SUBSCRIBE TO EVERYTHING WE PUBLISH

Do you love what Microcosm publishes?

Do you want us to publish more great stuff?

Would you like to receive each new title as it's published?

Subscribe as a BFF to our new titles and we'll mail them all to you as they are released!

$10-30/mo, pay what you can afford. Include your t-shirt size and your birthday for a possible surprise!

microcosmpublishing.com/bff

...AND HELP US GROW YOUR SMALL WORLD!

Other books about changing the world around you: